The Slippery Art
of Book Reviewing

By Mayra Calvani and
Anne K. Edwards

Twilight Times Books
Kingsport Tennessee

The Slippery Art of Book Reviewing

Twilight Times Books
P O Box 3340
Kingsport, TN 37664
http://twilighttimesbooks.com/

First Edition, June 2008

Library of Congress Cataloging-in-Publication Data

Calvani, Mayra.
The slippery art of book reviewing / by Mayra Calvani and Anne K. Edwards. -- 1st ed.
   p. cm.
ISBN-13: 978-1-933353-22-7 (trade pbk. : alk. paper)
ISBN-10: 1-933353-22-8 (trade pbk. : alk. paper)
1. Book reviewing. I. Edwards, Anne K., 1940- II. Title.
PN98.B7C25 2008
808'.066028--dc22
         2008010149

Cover art by Kurt Ozinga

Printed in the United States of America

Foreword by James A. Cox

When I began reviewing books for a small community sponsored public radio station in Madison, Wisconsin in the fall of 1976, providing literary critiques of published literature was largely the prerogative of an ivory tower elite primarily concentrated among the literati of New York City along with a few Ivory League bastions such as Boston and Philadelphia.

It was a time when publishing was dominated by the large New York publishing houses, with subsidized academic presses serving primarily as means for academics to secure tenure.

I began with an Underwood manual typewriter, a Rolodex of contact information for sixty of the largest publishing firms in the country, and some letterhead stationary with Madison Review of Books in the masthead.

At the same time, I began to supervise volunteers and adding their reviews to our weekly half-hour broadcasts, as well as corresponding with publishing house publicity and marketing departments providing them with copies of the reviews and soliciting new submissions.

In 1978 an additional platform was added to provide opportunities for the increasing number of reviewers and their reviews with the first weekly cable television show in Madison which I produced, hosted and aptly named 'Bookwatch.' It was to run for 21 years with the final program airing in December of 2001.

In 1980, because of our expanded geographic networks of reviewers and audiences, the Madison Review of Books was renamed the Midwest Book Review, with the first of what was to become nine monthly book review newsletters and magazines being launched.

Along the way additional platforms and forums for reviews were added including a short-wave radio broadcast that beamed reviews to all of the countries of the world. Our reviews became staples of such online book review databases as alt.bookreviews. com, Amazon.com, Lexus-Nexus, Goliath, and Book Review Index. The Midwest Book Review website was created for authors, publishers, librarians, booksellers, and the general reading public – becoming one of the largest and most respected of such sites in the publishing industry.

I began early on to give workshops and seminars on book reviewing and the setting up of book review organizations. Was the frequent subject of interviews with authors writing 'how to' books on writing, publishing for a book reviewer's perspective. With the advent of the Internet I often became an interviewed guest for podcasts when the subject of reviewing books was on the agenda.

Now in its third year, I also write a monthly column of commentary and advice for writers and publishers called the "Jim Cox Report."

This is basically how I came to acquire something of an expertise in reviewing books on a professional level and in a multiplicity of venues, forums, and formats. I've had the honor and responsibility for supervising, editing, and educating hundreds of people in the art, craft, and science of reviewing books.

Just as it is the mission of the Midwest Book Review to promote literacy, library usage, and small press publishing, I feel that it is the obligation of book reviewers, be they amateurs or professionals, to encourage with their reviews and critiques writers to write better, publishers to publish more effectively, and readers to read with greater satisfaction.

Toward these ends I wholeheartedly recommend that anyone who aspires to reviewing books effectively and responsibly needs to master the information, apply the advice, read carefully the recommendations, and take advantage of the resources to be found in Mayra Calvani and Anne K. Edwards' superbly organized and thoroughly 'user friendly' instruction manual "The Slippery Art of Book Reviewing."

There is far more to competently reviewing a work of fiction or a book of non-fiction than what we all remember from the turning out of book reports in our school days. "The Slippery Art of Book Reviewing" covers all the aspects of this detailed process providing not only the 'rules of the road' for reviewing books, but the reasoning behind those rules as well.

Also covered in depth is a practical approach to the nuts and bolts of operating a book review organization, publication, or website.

The three major problems that are commonplace among book reviewers is that of egregiously imposing their own egos upon their assessments of what they are reviewing; lacking an appropriate and consistent structure with respect to their workload; and failing to communicate effectively with the publishing community.

The first of these weaknesses is self-evident to us all. Reviewers who are reviewing the book they think should have been written instead of the one that was. Of preferring a well-crafted and malicious put-down to an honest but non-malicious critique of a book's weaknesses and strengths. Of failing to support their opinions with cited and exampled reasoning.

The second of these flaws emerges with such symptoms as failing to meet deadlines, becoming overwhelmed by the numbers of titles clamoring for attention, falling into the use of hack formulas rather than customized critiques.

The third of these problems is reflected by the absence of professional quality letterhead stationary; a failure to notify publishers of the reviews and to provide them with a copy of the review; and a chronic lack of accessibility or responsiveness to authors and publishers with respect to the status of their book submissions.

The cure for these commonly encountered book reviewer defects is simple and straight forward.

1. Write with a professional and justified detachment on the merits and demerits of the book within the framework of expectations focused upon the author's intended readership.

2. Treat book reviewing as the professional activity it should be, complete with daily, weekly, monthly schedules and project calendars; as well as dealing with solicited and unsolicited incoming titles submissions according to a coherent initial screening process, status inquiry response system, assignment tracking system, and realistic deadline schedule.

3. Always provide the authors, publishers, or publicists who submit review copies with a copy of the review along with a notification cover letter on professional letterhead stationary explaining where the review has been published or posted or broadcast.

In the end, the way to become an effective and respected book reviewer is the same process that professional musicians must apply to the mastery of their chosen instruments – practice, practice, practice.

One last piece of advice based upon decades of personal experience. If the reading of books has been your favored hobby and you seek to make your living (or some substantial portion of it) from reviewing what you read – then it is time for you to get a new hobby!

As for all of you who aspire to review books and to have your reviews made available to the widest possible readership I have only one final recommendation.

Read very carefully the following pages that comprise "The Slippery Art of Book Reviewing" – and keep it close by for future reference.

James A. Cox
Editor-in-Chief
Midwest Book Review

Contents

PART ONE
The Art of Reviewing

PART TWO
The Influence of Book Reviews

PART THREE
Resources

Preface

So You Want to Be a Reviewer?

Are you passionate about books? Do you have a talent for easily capturing the essence of a book after having read it? Do you often feel the desire to share your thoughts about a book with readers? If you answered "Yes" to these questions, then book reviewing can be one of the most satisfying, rewarding activities you'll ever undertake. In fact, book reviewing can become addictive.

I started reviewing in 1998. Back then, I wished someone had written a book with all there is to know about book reviewing. Sure, I found many articles on the web about the craft, which I read eagerly. But, I really wished I could have found everything in one volume. A sort of "user's manual"—a book that I would be able to come back to again and again and use as a reference, one that would reveal the secrets of the trade, the Dos and Don'ts, full of guidelines, tips and practical advice.

Though it may seem strange, there are hundreds of books on writing in general, and many on writing book reports, proposals, query letters and synopses, but practically none on writing reviews.

Like all fledgling reviewers, I made my share of amateurish mistakes, becoming all the more experienced and polished because of them. I, too, was guilty of the fledgling reviewer's disease—that of writing overly-positive reviews. Overwhelmed with enthusiasm, a good heart, and the desire to please everyone associated with the book, I often made the big mistake of forgetting the foremost person a reviewer must keep in mind— the reader. As I read and wrote more and more reviews, it soon became easy to tell a good review from a bad one, and to realize that a large number of reviewers, especially beginners, would profit from a bit of guidance, the things I learned from my mistakes.

The fact is, most people *do* read reviews to select their reading material. Reviews *do* have a positive or a negative influence on whether or not a person buys a book. Hence, reviewing is a serious responsibility, one reviewers shouldn't take lightly.

The aim of this book, therefore, is to offer some guidelines in a clear manner supported with targeted examples of how to write and publish thoughtful, well-written reviews no matter their length, type or genre, and to examine the essence of reviews within a broader spectrum.

This book was written not only with the aspiring reviewer in mind, but for the established reviewer who needs a bit of refreshing and also for anybody—be they author, publisher, reader, bookseller, librarian or publicist—who wants to become more informed about the value, purpose and effectiveness of reviews.

On a final note, the writing of this book has been a highly interesting, educational and thrilling ride into the slippery world of reviews for Anne K. Edwards and me. I hope you'll enjoy the journey and profit from it as much as we have.

So take out pen and paper, a highlighter, and get ready to write great reviews!

Mayra Calvani

Acknowledgments

This book wouldn't have been possible without all the professionals—authors, publishers, librarians, booksellers, publicists, book-review editors—who so generously took time to share their knowledge and answer our questions. To all of you, thank you.

To Lida Quillen for believing in our fledgling project.

A special thanks to Andrea Sisco, Tami Brady, and Maggie Ball for demystifying the process of how to start a book review site, and to Spanish linguist and translator Teresa Carbajal Ravet for all her valuable tips on reviewing translations.

PART ONE
The Art of Reviewing

The Five Keys to Being a Good Reviewer

In order to become a good reviewer, first and foremost, you'll need the following:

Command of Language

A solid command of English (or whatever language you write in). This includes a good knowledge of grammar, syntax, spelling and punctuation.

Let's face it. You might be able to express your thoughts clearly, but if your review has grammatical, spelling or punctuation mistakes, nobody will take you seriously. You might get away with posting your poorly-written review on Amazon or B&N, but no serious review site or publication will accept your review. Print publications, in particular, demand spotless submissions. Even if you have a word processor to take care of typos, this is usually never enough to correct grammatical or punctuation mistakes. Too many words pronounced the same way, like piqued, peaked, and peeked, end up being misused because this type of mistake is ignored by spellcheckers.

If you need some refreshing, get a good grammar book, take an English course in writing, or buy yourself a copy of Strunk and White's *The Elements of Style*, which continues to be a classic that all serious writers must have. Also, a good thesaurus should always be on a reviewer's desk.

Clarity of Thought

Likewise, you may have a solid command of the English language, but if you lack the ability to express your thoughts clearly, you won't be doing your job properly. A good review should sparkle with clarity. Keep your sentences straight and to the point. Follow a logical order when describing the plot and writing the evaluation. Don't let your thoughts stray all over the place or use unnecessary words. Each word you use in your review should count and have a purpose. Luckily, a good review has a specific structure which will be discussed in the *How To Write A Book Review* section. Sticking to this simple structure will help you keep your thoughts organized.

Honesty

Yes, the topic of honesty will keep appearing in different sections of this book for the simple reason that it is so often taken lightly by reviewers.

Honesty is what defines a reviewer's trade. Readers, who turn to reviews before purchasing a book, depend on this honesty. And ultimately, a reviewer's foremost—and probably *only*—obligation is to readers, not to authors and publishers. "A reviewer's honest judgment is his stock in trade. Without it, a review is little more than weak PR," says Maggie Ball, owner and book review editor of *The Compulsive Reader* (http://www.compulsivereader.com/html/index.php), an online publication that specializes in serious fiction and long, in-depth reviews.

Objectivity

According to Random House Webster's Dictionary, to be objective is to be "not influenced by personal feelings, unbiased."

What does this mean to you, the reviewer? Simply that, ideally, you shouldn't let your values, beliefs, and way of life influence your review.

Let's say that you detest abortion, but are assigned to review a book where the protagonist has one. You get angry as you read, and may even start planning in your mind a negative review in spite of the fact that the book is well written, the characters compelling, the descriptions evoking. In this case, to write a negative review would be wrong, unfair, and dishonest. If you succumb to your personal feelings, you're being subjective, and a good reviewer, to the best of his or her ability, is not supposed to be subjective.

Sticking to books with plots with which you feel comfortable is the best way to avoid this problem. If you detest violence, for instance, don't review books about serial killers. Chances are, your opinion will be biased.

Objectivity in reviewing is the deliberate ignoring of your personal biases and preferences in order to write an honest review based on all parts of a book—plot, writing, characterization, construction and so on. However, the objective review will become subjective when the reviewer sums up their observations of the book in a logical manner and recommends it or doesn't recommend it.

Remember, just because you don't like the book doesn't mean it is bad.

When writing an objective review, try to put your feelings aside. One effective way to handle this situation is to mention it in your review to those who might be offended by the book, as well as those who might like it—even if you don't!

Tact

What you say is as important as *how* you say it, and this is where tact comes in, especially when writing negative reviews.

Stating your thoughts tactfully and eloquently while offering examples to support your evaluation will keep the negative review from sounding harsh, mean, or insulting. Your aim is not to offend or humiliate the author, but clearly explain to the reader why this particular book is not worth reading. When you phrase your reviews tactfully, the authors themselves can learn and profit from your negative reviews.

Avoid statements like "This is a terrible book" or "This is the worst book I've ever read." This screams 'unprofessional' and will label you as an amateur. There are other statements you can use to convey your negative reaction to the book. For instance, the harsh phrases mentioned above can be replaced by, "This book didn't live up to its full potential because...." or "This novel didn't work for me for the following reasons..."

What is a Book Review?

A book review is many things to many people. It is a judgment, a recommendation, a criticism, a job, an ego booster, interpretation, retelling part of the story, and others. So when you ask what a review is, and what purpose it serves, you ask a simple question with a complex answer.

A book review is different to each person in its intent, the impact it has and the final communication between reader and reviewer.

A review is an ego booster to an author if the reviewer finds the book praiseworthy. To that same author, it is a promotion too. It also tells the author if they've achieved their goal in the writing of the book. The author learns if their book is considered well written, well plotted, well researched, interesting, and if the characters are real enough in the world they inhabit to hold the reader's attention. If the review faults the book on any one of these items, the review is a teaching/learning tool (depending on how the author receives it and if the reviewer writes fairly of the book). It proves to the author that they have or have not learned their craft.

To the reviewer, a review is the end result of reading a book. The reviewer must then decide on the content of the review which will depend on where the review is going, who will read it, the length the recipient prefers, and if the recipient prefers positively-worded reviews only. Some reviews will be negative no matter how a reviewer tries to word them because there are one or more major faults they found in the book. This dictates what the reviewer will say in the review. So, for a reviewer, a review is a two-step communication, reviewer to author/recipient, and through them to the reader.

A reviewer does not just write a review and that is the end of it. Each review a reviewer writes has an impact on the reviewer's reputation as well as the author's. Too much praise for any book and the reader may be suspicious that the reviewer is either a friend of the author or afraid to write even a little critically of an author's work. Too much negativity in a review has the same effect. It either causes one to suspect the reviewer of playing god to build up his own ego or having an ax to grind. It may reflect the reviewer's inability to understand the message of the book, or the story, or their lack of knowledge of how to write a fair review. Some reviewers think they must find fault with every book they read.

To a reader who uses reviews to gather information about new books, a review is a source of information. They must be able to trust the reviewer's judgment as they are spending money and time on this book. If they believe a recommendation by a reviewer and find, upon reading the book, the reviewer did not tell what they, the reader, considers to be the truth or that the reviewer was only helping the author or publisher sell books, they will not trust that reviewer again. Thus, the reviewer's reputation suffers, and soon, no one will take their word as worth anything. Although the author may continue to solicit reviews from this reviewer to use for promotion of a book in which case, the reviewer isn't a reviewer, but has become a promotional blurb writer.

A review is a messenger that spreads the word about the book to publications, libraries, booksellers, websites and so forth. It may say anything from how much a reviewer enjoyed the book to how much they disliked the book and all that falls in between those two extremes. There are many publications in print that carry reviews and many websites that post them. Some of the publications and websites take reviews very seriously and have staff who do the reviews. Others accept freelance reviews written by satisfied readers.

A review tells a reader if the book is worth the time or not, keeping in mind that not all books fall into the area of interest of all reviewers. For instance, if a reviewer who loves romance but hates violence reads a mystery thriller or a horror story, their review may be negative because of the violence contained in the book. But if that same reviewer reads a story about two people finding true love in spite of seemingly insurmountable odds, they would probably recommend it highly if it were well written. Like other readers, reviewers have their preferences and that often shows in their reviews which recommend or don't recommend a work.

A review also tells the world there's a new book on the horizon that might be worth investigating, a chance to experience something new, to learn something not known, to see new worlds through the eyes of the writer. A well-written review may lure the reader into a new genre, thus opening a new market for that genre's writers and giving that reader a set of new places to visit and new people to meet.

Reviews that are well written offer much to the reading world, they carry information about the book, the author and the reviewer. A poorly-written review offers the same information, but may turn readers from exploring the book, future works of that author, or turn them against recommendations by this reviewer. Thus, a review can have a lasting effect on an author or reviewer's career. This, in turn, affects the publisher who may not be willing to submit any other works to that reviewer's incompetence.

It all boils down to reviews having a far-reaching effect. Like a stone dropped into a pond the ripples do spread outward, even though one may be almost unaware of them. It is a gamble for an author or publisher to ask someone to write a review of their work, an extension of the same risk they take in putting the time into writing the book or the money a publisher invests in putting the book on the market. Positive reviews help produce positive results for all concerned if the book is truly worth a reader's time and money.

An overly-positive review about a poorly-written book is a cheat in any way it is viewed. It misinforms the reader, perhaps causing them to buy a book they won't enjoy or that is even unreadable, it tells the publisher that an author who hasn't learned their craft is a good writer, and it tells the author that they have done a good job when they haven't.

"Some authors should never be published and I think it's a reviewer's responsibility to critique to that extent," says Ron Kavanaugh, publisher of *Mosaic* (http://www.mosaicbooks.com), a print review publication specializing in African-American and Latin-American literature. "Assuming that every-thing—publisher, writer, reviewer, bookseller, and reader—is connected, then not to review books honestly is to perpetuate a bad writer's career, lessening the chances that a decent writer may be published instead."

Some reasons for overly-positive reviews are because the reviewer is afraid to write anything negative or doesn't want to hurt an author's feelings or because the media or website publishing the review only wants positive reviews. Another reason is that the reviewer may be afraid of facing criticism that may be turned on them for anything other than such a review. For some reviewers it is hard to say something negative in a positive fashion and yet warn the reader that this may not be a book worth taking home. Thus, the reader wastes his time and money on a poorly-written book because of a review that was written in false terms.

Reviews are harbingers of good things to come for a reader, author, and publisher if a book is well done. The review tells the world this book deserves to be read, the author deserves to be known and the publisher deserves to sell that book. Reviews introduce new authors to the world and encourage readers to buy their books, thus helping to build that writer's reputation.

Reviews are sounding boards for reviewers to tell the world why some books should be read and why others should not. A satisfied reviewer will write a satisfied review and recommend the book to others.

Reviews are tools used by booksellers, libraries, and even publishers. Booksellers peruse reviews online and in print publications to make decisions on what to stock on their shelves. Libraries use them for the same reason and may keep them on hand for their readers to read. Some readers will ask the library to get a certain book based on reviews they've seen. And publishers may use reviews as feedback in helping decide whether or not the next book by this author is worth publishing.

A review can be many things to one person or one thing to many people. It depends on the reviewer and the reader of that review. Some reviewers are academics and write very thoughtfully-constructed reviews of varying lengths that offer an in-depth look at the content and perhaps the message of a book. Their reviews will not be read by the average reader nor will their reviews be about books the average reader would likely peruse as they are meant to reach readers in a specific field of interest or profession. This review, while very informative to the reviewer's peers, may appear too wordy or dull to someone not interested or acquainted with that book's subject matter. Yet, that same review will be perfectly aimed at the intended readership.

While a review by an academic may not work for the average reader, nor is such a review likely to be the result of the average reviewer's work, it serves to let a portion of the world know about the work of a specific author whose work might be of interest to those who work in that field and serves notice to the author that their work is considered worth the time of their intended audience.

This is how reviews work. They spread the word about books, authors and publishers, serve to alert the reading world of their existence and give a leg-up to an author's career. Reviews grab a reader's attention and say "Read this book" or "Don't read this book." Reviews are part of the cycle of publishing a book, helping to link reader to author, which, in the end, is their purpose.

Reading Critically

In order to write thoughtful, intelligent reviews, whether short or long, it is important and highly recommended that you learn to read critically. This doesn't necessarily mean that reading has to become a task, or that keeping a critical eye open during reading will take the "joy" out of reading. Though it may seem like work at first, once you get used to reading critically, you will do it automatically and will be able to enjoy the book just as if you weren't consciously keeping track of its good and bad qualities.

Though different reviewers work in different ways, good reviewers usually have a pencil or a highlighter in hand to take key notes or mark important lines or passages they may want to refer to later while writing the review. This is especially true in the case of long, in-depth reviews. If you don't want to write or mark the book, then keeping a notebook for notes is a great idea. You can jot down clue words as you read along, or write down any page numbers you plan to quote from. If you don't like the idea of taking notes while reading, then another choice is to stick Post-its ™ on the particular pages that got your attention—this way you don't have to stop to write, nor damage the book.

Taking notes is helpful for remembering the names, ages and professions of the characters, as well as the locations or main points of the storylines. It is human to forget, especially when reading long novels with many characters and subplots, and taking notes will keep the information straight and fresh in your mind. You want to make sure you don't make mistakes about the book or get the facts wrong when writing the review. This is the signature of an amateur and an obvious sign that the reviewer didn't give the proper amount of time or importance to the book. Don't forget you have a responsibility to whoever sent you the book, be it author, publisher, or review-site moderator, to write a careful, well-thought-out review. After all, you're not only getting a free book, but these people (especially in the case of paperbacks or hardbacks) paid a substantial amount of postage to have the book sent to you. For those reviewers who live overseas, the cost is even higher.

If you're an author as well as a reviewer, reading critically will become a learning experience. You'll be able to understand what works and what doesn't, what unusual techniques to try, as well as common pitfalls to avoid when writing your own books.

In order to read critically, be aware of the following points as you move through the book, taking notes as seems necessary.

Plot

- Setting time and location.
- Characters' names, ages, and professions.
- Write down the main plot points.
- Is the plot original? Has it been done many times? If not original, is it written from a fresh angle?
- Are there any unusual techniques or plot twists?

Narrative and Flow

- Does the prose flow smoothly?
- Are there abrupt changes of tense, speakers, subject matter, setting, etc., which distract the reader?
- Are the paragraphs light and short, or heavy and long?
- Is the language evocative?
- Are any clichés used?
- Are adverbs used too often?
- Is there too much telling instead of letting the characters talk to the reader?
- Are any redundancies included, either with words, characters, effects or situations?
- Any memorable lines (particularly funny, scary, witty, dark, insightful, etc.) for potential quotes?

Pacing

- Is it slow and boring, or so quick and exciting you can't stop reading? (Keep in mind that sometimes a book may be slow, yet fascinating at the same time. Likewise, the pace might be fast, yet the story might be poorly written. In other words, fast paced doesn't necessarily mean good.)
- Does the author stop the story to give too much detailed information about a character's job, making the book read like a technical manual?

Characterization

- Are the characters stereotyped or so real they make you feel they're genuine people?
- Do the characters act realistically in all situations?
- Are their actions and reactions believable?
- Do the characters act in accordance with their natures or personalities as established?
- What about secondary characters? (Sometimes these can really stand out.)

Dialogue

- Is it stilted or natural?
- Does it sparkle with crispness or is it repetitive and boring?
- Does the author talk down to the reader by adding self-evident explanations to the dialogue?
- Do the characters regurgitate what the readers already know? (Too much telling.)

Description

- Is there too much description, so that it halts the flow of the story? Too little? None at all?
- What sense does it convey?
- Are there any unforgettable or unusual images?

- Is the prose bloated with adjectives?
- Does the author describe emotions that have been described previously in the dialogue? (Again, too much telling.)

Symbolism and Allegories

- Are there any recurrent symbols used throughout the book? Any allusions?
- Are similes and metaphors clear and effective?

Point of View

- How is the point of view? Is the story told in the first person? The third? Author omniscient? Various combinations?
- Does the author jump from one point of view to another in a way that disrupts the reader's suspension of disbelief?

Theme

- What is the theme? Is it universal?

Tone and Atmosphere

- Is there a distinct tone or atmosphere that permeates the book throughout? Dream-like? Spooky? Mysterious? Funny?

Spelling and Grammar

- Is the book well edited?
- Does it have grammatical, spelling or punctuation mistakes?

When reading nonfiction books, you should also be aware of the following, taking notes as necessary.

- Author's qualifications. Is the author well qualified to write about the subject? Is he/she an expert, scholar, medical doctor or PhD? If the author graduated from a top school like Harvard or MIT, for instance, it should be mentioned in the review.

- What is the author trying to accomplish? Inform? Teach? Persuade? Entertain? Is the author successful in achieving his/her goal?

- Are the ideas structured in a way that is clear, or does it jump from one topic to another confusingly?

- Does the author use charts, diagrams, pictures, statistics or quotes from famous people to support, illustrate and prove his point?

- Is the author objective in presenting his case? No author writing a research book presenting new evidence or ground-breaking ideas can afford to allow emotions to get in the way of whatever statements they make or whatever proof they are offering. They must use facts to back up whatever they say and set it up in such a way as to convince the reader this is information worth considering and accepting. If there is any hint of emotionalism, arrogance, or guesswork in the writing, it means the author has allowed his ego to creep into the work and lost his objectivity. This statement is based on the idea that anyone conducting research knows they may not achieve the results they sought, and they may discover they need more facts before writing a paper to inform the rest of the scientific world of their work or conclusions. This can only be done by being objective in the research and the resulting paper. This is true for any research being conducted. In research, objectivity is the key.

- Is the book a light, joyful read or heavy and difficult? (Light and joyful doesn't necessarily mean better, and the heavy, difficult book can be the better read—just look at the classics!)

- Who is the audience for the book? Is this a book that can be read by most people, or only by readers who are already familiar with the topic?

Reviewers shouldn't review nonfiction books about subjects they don't understand. Not being familiar with a subject leads to weak evaluations and to reviews that won't be helpful to readers. The same holds true for poetry and plays. Any reviewer needs to be grounded in the art form to be reviewed or they shouldn't undertake it. They must be able to read for hidden meanings, symbolism, and so forth with a true knowledge of the subject. They should not automatically approach any work with questions, negative feelings, or instant dislike of the subject matter or form used by the author. This is loss of objectivity and produces a negative and often unfair review. So a reviewer must look for the objectivity of the author as well as his own in reading this type of work for review. If the reviewer comes to any paper or body of information on any research with feelings of being unable to accept anyone else's work in this field that does not echo their own, they will not be able to give a fair or objective review. Most likely, their review will be negative.

Keeping all these points in mind as you read may seem overwhelming in the beginning, but as you review more and more books, your mind will become conditioned and trained, and you'll be able to absorb all of it as easy as A, B, C.

How to Write a Book Review

First, read the book.

Then, keeping in mind the points made under the section entitled *Reading Critically*, decide how you want to slant the review and what you want to say.

The use of the term 'slant' means the angle or approach you want to use in writing the review. Will it be negative, positive, enthusiastic, glowing, or so full of praise that it sounds overdone? Those are some of the choices you have. And regardless of what type of review you write, you must be able to back up all criticisms or praises with points from the book, including editing, writing, plotting, and character development. Otherwise, your integrity as a reviewer is in jeopardy.

- Negative reviews encompass the width and depth of a reviewer's reactions to a book resulting from poor writing, characterization or plot flaws to the failure of editors and publishers to make sure the book is the best it can be. Ideally, all criticisms should be backed up by examples.

- Positive reviews include all the reviewer's reactions that fall on the plus side, i.e., the good writing, the good character development, the good plotting. It also includes editing done by author and editor and proofing by the publisher to turn out a well-done book.

- Enthusiastic reviews fall into the category of a reviewer really enjoying the book and just having to tell the world how good or how great it was. All points made by a reviewer in this category should also be backed up by examples.

Once the reviewer has chosen an approach, the next decision is how to get the reader to read the review and perhaps, then, the book. We call this a 'hook.' A hook is any set of words that will attract a reader and hold their attention long enough to get them to read the complete review. Without something to catch a reader's eye, the review goes unread or may be set aside, and this means the reviewer's work is wasted, the communication between reviewer and reader broken.

The hook might be, for instance, a question like: "How would you like to travel on a space ship?" This sets the general subject and genre of the book in the same line. In this case the subject would be space travel and the genre would be science fiction, though it might also fall into the futuristic sub-genre, depending on the plot.

Other forms of hooks might be positive statements such as "A keeper! An exciting story about murder in an old English castle," or "Get out your hiking boots and join the characters in this exciting story of adventures of the heart." In both of these cases the subject and genre are mentioned, giving the reader vital information and, hopefully, luring them into reading the rest of the review.

A non-hook is the rather flat beginning such as "This is a story about two people who meet and fall in love." This type of opening or non-hook is often (though not always) used by reviewers who didn't find the story exciting or well written enough to be interesting and alerts the reader to that fact. It also gives the subject and genre in case the reader might be interested in reading further.

Other types of hooks are often used and each reviewer may invent his or her own. For instance, sometimes a particularly interesting quote from the book may serve as the hook. Failure to interest and hold the reader is the fault of the reviewer.

A reviewer must be ready to accept responsibility for his or her words about a book. Never write a review that disparages the book just because you think this will build you a reputation as a tough reviewer. This really points to the reviewer not having any idea what reviews are about and will erode your credibility. Authors, publishers and booksellers will not ask you to do reviews for them.

Never write a review demeaning another author's work if you are an author and feel some envy because this author managed to write a book that turns out better in one way or another than your own. Instead of reacting with hostility, this is the time to give due credit to that author and use what you've learned from reading their book to make your own work better. No one knows everything about writing so if a reviewer reads with an open mind, their reviews will show it and their reputation will be enhanced.

Reviews are written using certain constructions. This will depend on where you are posting the review or what site it is written for or the print media that will be using it. Each review publisher, whether print media or an online site, has their own requirements and a reason for those requirements. If your review does not conform to them, it will not be accepted and you have lost an opportunity. Some review editors prefer short, light reviews, claiming that readers have short attention spans and a million things to do, while others prefer long, in-depth reviews. Some prefer summary reviews instead of critical reviews, believing that a critical review leaves no room for the readers to make their own decisions.

"There are different kinds of reviews," says James Cox, editor of *Midwest Book Review* (http://www.midwestbookreview.com). "Librarians and bookstore retailers who have limited time find that short, succinct reviews have the most practical value for them. Academia and the general reading public prefer to have reviews of greater length—because they will both have the time and the interest in a more definitive analysis."

Whether short or long, the favorite 'formula' seems to be an interesting lead/hook, a brief summary, and an evaluation.

Alex Moore, editor-in-chief of *Foreword Magazine* (http://www.forewordmagazine.com), states, "The structure I prefer is: good lead (an interesting anecdote, a good quote, an amazing fact, or significant statement), summary of contents but not to give away the ending in fiction, author's credentials, two-three specific examples through detail and description of the author's criticism/comments, conclusion with a hoped-for flourish or connecting tether to the opening. Approximately 450 words."

Most review publishers do not want negative reviews that are written just to be fault finding. They may accept them if they also include some positive points or are written in a language that is clear but not hostile or critical.

Some review publishers want very short reviews due to space constraints, so the review must be concise—less than 200 words. These review publishers like to see a brief two-or-so lines about what the plot is, comments on the writing, a brief opinion of the author and an opening with a definite hook. An example of this type of review would be found in *Library Journal* (http://www.libraryjournal.com), one of the top pre-release review publications aimed at librarians.

The review publishers that use the longer reviews want to see a good hook, a longer opinion about the writing backed up with quotes or examples of what the reviewer means, and a critique of the writing, plot, characterization, setting, and style. They also want a general breakdown of the plot that does NOT ever include the ending. This breakdown should be just enough to whet the appetite of the reader for more.

Publishers of academic reviews usually want reviews from people who know the field that the book is about. They will want discussions of the qualities or lack of qualities of the book, including whether or not the data used really proves the point the author is trying to make. They will also want discussions about where the book stands compared to others in the field or within the author's body of work.

There are also reviews of nonfiction books that fall into so many areas, it is impossible to mention them all. The reviews for these books will use the same basic elements such as naming the particular area the book falls into, such as lifestyle, self-help, how-to books, and so forth.

Any reviewer worth his salt will know their genre or field before they attempt to review a book. Reviewing outside your area of interest or expertise will require research if you aren't familiar with the subject of the book or the field.

Once a reviewer has decided on angle of approach to the review and what they want to say, their review will need to follow certain basic guidelines that apply to all reviews.

These include:

Clarity of Expression

- Use words that all readers can understand. Keep the sentences short and straightforward. Do not try to be obtuse by using references with which the average person wouldn't be familiar.

Understand how a book is constructed

Understand the major themes, characterization, tone, plot and pace. These are some of the foundation blocks in fiction and a reviewer should be able to identify them. (See *Reading Critically*).

- A book consists of three parts—the beginning where all the characters are introduced (there may be a few minor exceptions here), the plot is stated and begun, the tone of the book is set, and action must commence. Then comes the middle that is often considered filler, but in fact serves to continue the action from the beginning through to the end. It is here that many authors, both new and experienced, get bogged down and must slog or bluff their way through, but it is really where the characters struggle the most with the mounting problems they face and suffer their setbacks.

The ending is where all loose ends are tied off, the characters find a solution to their problem and the story reaches its conclusion. The ending must be logical and never hurried or abrupt. No author should introduce a new character to "suddenly" either be the villain or solve the problem.

The three parts are not the same length and vary from writer to writer and from book to book.

- Depending on the book, the major themes may be something like: love conquers in the end (as in romance fiction), crime doesn't pay, the corruption of nobility, the hypocrisy of religious people, the shallowness of the upper classes, good overcomes evil, evil conquers good (as in most horror fiction), not all stories have happy endings, etc. A theme is not a subject in a story, but a broad idea or message conveyed by it. Often a theme is universal and deals with life, society or human nature.

- Characterization is the process of creating characters and allowing them to speak and grow. Does the author waste a lot of time describing them with blocks of words? This is the mark of an amateur.

Does the author constantly tell the reader what the character thinks instead of letting the character tell the reader? Phrases like "he felt", "he thought", "he wanted", will indicate author intrusion here. If there is only a rare use of these phrases, the author is letting the character tell the reader (though author telling is often done in author omniscient person) or narrative fiction.

This is where the character reveals himself or herself gradually, by letting the reader know how they feel, think, or act. It is really just a matter of a few words and the way they are used that shows whether or not the author is doing the telling.

The name an author chooses for a character generally reveals something about the character. The way they walk, talk, sit, and dress are also devices authors will use. For instance, a gossipy character who seems too friendly might be shown as beginning her conversation with questions that are none of her business, or opening with a whispered comment as an aside to another character about someone else's poor taste in dress, or unfortunate habit of being late, or having gained weight around the waist, or that a male character is paying too much attention to a married woman, or that he has been seen coming out of a 'house of ill repute'.

- The tone of the book is that overall sense of atmosphere a reader gets from the reading of it. If it is a gothic horror, the atmosphere will seem consistently dark and threatening, if it is a romantic comedy, the atmosphere will seem light-hearted and fun. This is something a reviewer must recognize to place the book in its proper genre when discussing its merits or lack thereof and whether it meets the basic requirements of its particular genre.

- The plot is the way the events are structured in a story. It is bound by the laws of cause and effect. A plot answers these questions about the story—what if? (the premise), who? (the protagonist), what's at stake? (the conflict), how? (how does the protagonist solve the problem or overcome the obstacles), how does it end? (the resolution). Ideally, a good plot rises in intensity until the climax (more exciting part of the story) and then descends into the conclusion or ending. A reviewer should be able to tell the signs of a poorly-plotted book, or a book with no plot. Does the story lack a climax? Do events contradict themselves? This often happens when there are logic problems in the plot. Are all questions answered by the end of the book? Do the first half and second half of the book seem to be inconsistent or unbalanced?

- The reviewer must be able to judge the pacing of a book. Since some books sag and slow down in the middle while characters are trying to understand what is happening to them or around them, the reviewer must be able to identify this in order to comment on it. Or, if the action is swift-moving from beginning to end with no pauses or breaks in tension, the reviewer should notice this. Or is the pacing slow and easy overall? Or does the tension rise and fall like ripples? Does the writing flow without abrupt changes in point of view or subject? Has the writer successfully connected one segment of the book, one paragraph to the other?

- A reviewer must be able to identify the readership for any book. For instance, a mystery containing gory scenes or a romance containing explicit sex scenes would be slanted toward the adult reader. This can be judged by the age of the main character or detective, the subject matter, the writing standards of the time period the book was written, or whatever genre the publisher/author has assigned to the work. If the character or detective solving the crime is under eighteen, this is generally a book that would appeal to the younger set. It is mostly a matter of the reader's reading preference, but they often identify with the characters and a young adult might not understand how an older character thinks or why they react as they do in certain situations. The reviewer should consider this as a matter of life experience and perception based on of having lived that experience. A twenty-five-year-old could not talk about World War One as a personal experience, but only from reading or seeing films of the historical standpoint would they understand anything about it.

  However, a person in their fifties and beyond would have more knowledge about this particular event because they might have heard their parents or grandparents talk about their own experiences during that war and how it affected them. The direct result from that war would have affected that generation and this in turn would filter down in some way to the next generation. For example, many people raised in the Great Depression years had little money, no jobs, and were forced to often beg for help. Those who had money in any amount would have made it stretch, no matter how much they had. This, in later years, might make their children consider them miserly because they went without luxuries and told their children if they wanted spending money to find a way to make some, like collecting bottles with a return deposit or delivering newspapers. So when the children of the post-Depression era reached adulthood, they might indulge in using credit for most purchases and wind up carrying a debt that would have frightened their parents. Thus, one generation would not understand another's desire to enjoy the good things "now" instead of saving for them, and vice versa.

Understanding that there are different life experiences or lack thereof a reader brings to reading a book helps a reviewer identify the intended readership of a book so they can write an accurate review aimed at that group.

- Another thing a reviewer must remember is to never give the ending away. This spoils the book for anyone who reads the review and in turn does a disservice to the author and publisher.

Remember, in writing a review, you are taking on a responsibility to recommend a book or not recommend it and why or why not someone should get the book. Those people, who use reviews to decide whether a book is for them, are looking to your review as a guide. A well-written review serves them well. After all, the reviewer's duty is to the reader first.

How to Review Audio Books, Graphic Novels and Works in Translation

When reviewing audio books, graphic novels and works in translation, the reviewer should keep in mind a few additional factors beyond the ones already mentioned.

Audio Books

Audio books are books read aloud and recorded to be used in a listening device or player. For many people, especially the visually impaired, listening to audio books is the next best thing to reading print books. With audio books, the overall listening experience becomes almost as important as the book itself. For this reason, sometimes the book is edited for the audio version. For example, long descriptions in the original book may be shortened in order to make the audio book read better.

- How is the quality of the sound/recording? Is it clear?
- Is the narrator's voice suitable for the genre and mood of the story? Is it pleasing to the ears or annoying? What about the characters' voices and intonations?
- What about the background music and special effects (footsteps, knock on doors, wind, etc.)?
- Was the overall listening experience pleasurable?
- Has the book been shortened for the audio version or has it remained unabridged?

Graphic Novels

Graphic novels are similar to children's picture books in that there's very little text in them and the artwork is as important as the words. Each word must count and each illustration must add something new to the story.

- Does each small line of text add something new to the story?
- Is the prose and dialogue crisp and tight?
- How is the artwork?
- Are the illustrations evoking enough? Does the artist's style suit the genre?
- Is the artwork versatile or repetitive?
- Do the story and artwork complement each other?

Works in Translation

If you're reviewing a work in translation but you're not fluent in the language in which the original text was written, you may review the book just as if you were reviewing any other book. However, you should state in your review that you're only evaluating the story and *not* the translation. A full review of a work in translation requires the reviewer to be thoroughly knowledgeable in both languages in which the original book and the translation were written as well as familiar with the art of translation. Only then can the reviewer assess the translation and the work of the translator. A translation is a complex process in which the translator tries to express the meaning of context of one language into a second language as closely as possible. When translating, the meaning must remain the same. Unfortunately, this isn't always the case with translated works.

- Has the translator paid close attention to the context, meaning, and connotations of both languages?
- Has the translator kept in mind the author's writing style?
- Every language has its own writing conventions (punctuation, capitalization, grammar, and paragraphing). Has the translator paid close attention to these?

- Has the translator done a good job with idioms and popular phrases? Some idioms can't be translated literally into a second language.
- Has the translator used the correct form of points and commas when writing numbers? Even with English and Spanish decimals are written in different ways.

"Reviewers should mention, at the very least, that the work is a translation and mention the translator's name and background," states Teresa Carbajal Ravet (http://www.sententiavera.com), Spanish Linguist & Member of American Translators Association (ATA) andAmerican Literary Translators Association (ALTA). "Although reviewers may not be fluent in the original language of the book, they are capable of addressing 'matters of style, coherence, and narrative tone.' In simpler terms, is the language irregular (choppy) and is there distinction between characters' voices? These aspects of a translated book would certainly be issues of the translation and should be addressed in the review."

For more information on how to review translated works, Carbajal Ravet recommends reading the article, "Reviewing Guidelines for Translated Works" from the PEN American Center website at http://www.pen.org/page.php/prmID/269. Another helpful article she recommends, also written by ATA member Anne Milano Appel to ATA's *Chronicle*, is "Reviewing Translated Literature - Through a Glass Darkly?" XXXIV:8, Aug. 2005, 29-35. Interested reviewers may read this article on Milano's website at http://home.att.net/~amappel/index.htm. Click on 'Portfolio' and the link will take you to her publication list.

The Star System: Rating Books

When posting your reviews on sites like Amazon, for instance, you'll be asked to give a rating to the book—from one to five stars, five being the highest rating. This is often the same case with other review sites. More unusual, but still used, is the request to rate the book anywhere from one to ten.

Since no book fits just one category, sometimes it is difficult for reviewers to decide how many stars to give a book. Most books have a flaw in one place or another. Only a few are good enough to earn a 5 rating. It's easier, when possible, to have the choice of using halves, like 4 ½ stars, 3 ½ stars, and so on.

The following is a general guideline to help explain the rating system.

- 5 stars. Outstanding. Compelling plot and characterization. The writing sparkles. This is a book you won't soon forget (though bad books are difficult to forget, too!) and one you'll be eager to recommend to other readers.

- 4 stars. Good to very good. The plot and characterization may still be compelling, but the book itself, as a whole, doesn't 'sizzle' as much as the first. It is a book to enjoy, but one that you wouldn't recommend as strongly as the 5-star book.

- 3 stars. Mediocre to fairly good. This is the kind of book that has its share of both good and bad qualities. Maybe the plot is intriguing but it lacks characterization. It may have inconsistencies. Maybe it has a great hero or heroine to carry the story but the plot is weak. Perhaps there are a few spelling mistakes which might put you off, but not enough to quit reading. All in all, this is a book that, in spite of its weaknesses, is entertaining enough to keep you reading.

- 2 stars. Poor. Poorly written. Poorly edited. A poorly-executed plot and practically no characterization. Full of inconsistencies. A book you might want to toss in the trash before you're done with it.

- 1 star. Terrible. A book not worth reading. Badly written, clearly not edited at all, and filled with spelling and grammatical mistakes and/or with a very badly-constructed plot, no characterization, stilted dialogue. The author of this book clearly lacks the basic knowledge of the rules and elements of writing. A book that should have never been published, and one that you won't be able to keep reading after a couple of chapters.

There are other types of ratings for books. For romance books, for instance, reviewers are sometimes required to give a rating based on the level of sensuality in the book. This is useful for readers who might be offended by highly-explicit or 'steamy' scenes, or for those who would be bored by sweet romance. Different romance review sites have different rating guidelines. It is up to the reviewer to check the guidelines for the review site for which they're reviewing. Most often, sensuality ratings are given using hearts, ribbons or roses. On a scale of 1 to 5, a sweet romance may have a rating of 1 rose, while a very steamy one which isn't overly explicit may have a rating of 4 ½ roses, and so on.

Types of Reviews

Example of a Short Review and Breakdown

In writing a review, be sure to take into consideration the number of words the site or publisher wants or the limit on the number of words they will accept. Consider the depth of information about the book and perhaps the author they want. Study the type of reviews they use before writing your review. Some sites are very space conscious, others not so much. Print media also are of two minds, some accepting and preferring the longer, in-depth review, some preferring the shorter, more to-the-point review. Each will have their own limits on the number of words they will accept. Short reviews usually run from 250 to 450 words, with reviews of children's books at the lower end.

Be sure to include marketing information such as:

Title:
Author(s):
Publisher:
Copyright:
ISBN:
Format: (hardback, trade paperback, mass market paperback, ebook)
Genre:
State if the book is part of a series. Example: Book II in the...
Series.

(Other information, like publisher's address and full contact information, page count and price, may be required by the review site or publisher of the review.)

Some sites want a numerical rating as 1 (a lousy book) through to 5 (an excellent book) or they use stars or another symbol for the same type of rating.

Start the review with a hook such as:

Do you like hiking? (This catches the reader's attention and leads into the next line that sets the action and setting, in this case the age of dinosaurs.) Put on your hiking boots, grab up your backpack and join (characters' names) for a jaunt into the back country of (place name) and back into a time when dinosaurs roamed the Earth. (This information tells the reader what genre the book fits into).

(Characters' names) discover this is more than just a scientific trip to study early life forms as they find themselves searching for traces of a scientist who came to this same time and place and never returned. (This paragraph would contain the names of at least two of the main characters and the purpose of their trip. Here one may also include a bit about the plot.)

Talented author (name) takes us back to a time in our history where the Earth will tremble under our feet as volcanoes and hot geysers erupt. We'll smell the sulfur and feel the ash trickle down upon us as we hide from marauding dinosaurs. The tension is almost unbearable at times as we wait to see if we'll reach safety, so deeply will we be immersed in the story. Who among their traveling companions wants to keep them from doing their job? Why? (This third paragraph should perhaps include a bit about the writing, the setting, the action/plot, and characterization. As said before, never give away the ending or tell the reader anything that will give them the ending.)

This is a tale that is bound to please anyone with a sense of adventure, a time-travel fan who loves stories set in Earth's early years, or any reader who just dearly loves a fine yarn. Highly recommended by a very satisfied reader, though one who is exhausted from fleeing that tyrannosaurus rex. Enjoy. I sure did. (The last paragraph should include a bit of praise and a recommendation.)

Reviewed by (Reviewer's name)

Note: The reviewer's name may also be placed after the book's information and right before the actual review.

The above is a positive review with praise for the story. Let's take a look at what the final review would be like (this is not a real book, however, just an example).

Title: Day of King Rex
Author: Samuel D. Smith
Publisher: ABC Press and Company
(If required: Publisher's website/email/full address)
Copyright: January 2007
ISBN: 000-0000-00000-0-0
Format: Trade paperback (if required, page count and price may be added here)
Genre: Time Travel
Part of Series: Yes or No
Rating: (number from 1 to 10, or number from 1 to 5, or a count of stars from 1 to 5 may be required by some sites)

Do you like hiking? Then put on your hiking boots, grab up your backpack and join Harry Dean, Tommy James, Saul Moberg, and Marie Kareen for a jaunt into the back country of Wiscosicos Island off the coast of Maine and back into a time when dinosaurs roamed the Earth.

The time travelers, led by Harry Dean, find this is more than just a scientific trip to study early life forms as they discover their orders also include searching for traces of a paleobotanist who came to this same time and place and never returned. Harry Dean splits them into two pairs, assigning Marie Kareen to search with Tommy James while he and Saul Moberg investigate some caves they've found. Shortly after they separate, Marie is heard screaming. Harry and Saul rush to where they find her standing over the mangled body of Tommy James. It is some time before they can make sense of the warning she keeps repeating. Convinced a dinosaur attacked Tommy and Marie's garbled words are meaningless, the two men decide to take her with them and resume their search for the missing scientist.

Talented author Samuel D. Smith takes us back to a time in our history where the Earth will tremble under our feet as volcanoes and hot geysers erupt. We'll smell the sulphur and feel the ash trickle down upon us as we hide with Harry's party from marauding dinosaurs. The tension is almost unbearable at times as we wait to see if we'll reach safety, so deeply will we be immersed in the story. Who among the travelers wants to keep the party from doing its job? Why? This is a fast-moving and action-packed tale that will have you looking for other books by author Samuel D. Smith.

This is a tale that is bound to please anyone with a sense of adventure, a time-travel fan who loves stories set in Earth's early years, or any reader who just dearly loves a fine yarn. Highly recommended by a very satisfied reader, though one who is exhausted from fleeing that tyrannosaurus rex. Enjoy. I sure did.

Reviewed by Anne K. Edwards

(The reviewer's name may also appear after the book's information and right before the actual review.)

If you did not find the book you are writing the review about to be enjoyable, first consider why your reaction isn't favorable. Was the book poorly written in some way, boring or just not your preferred type of reading? Any time you feel a bias against a book, you must understand why before tackling the review. A reviewer must be objective and honest, able to back up any criticism they have of a book.

If the book is poorly written, your review might read something like:

This tale is about two scientists who travel back in time to the age of dinosaurs to conduct studies of that period. **(There is no hook in a negative review, because you are not telling readers this is a good book. Unless you are writing in a middle ground, you will be just delivering a general idea of what the book is about.)**

They soon learn they are also to conduct a search for a missing scientist who visited this same time period, but never returned. Subsequent time-travelers could find no trace of him or his camp. **(These two sentences set the genre and time of the story as well as what the book is about.)**

Characters' (names) are attacked and chased by several of the flesh-eating monsters that inhabit this period and, instead of being able to carry out their work, they must spend their time finding places of safety. (Female character name) slips and falls, winding up with a sprained ankle, thus proving she is only a token woman in this adventure while (male character's name) spends his time in long speeches about how he'll get them back safely. **(While this paragraph gives an idea of the plot, it also tells the reader that the author has used stereotyped characters and the plot is unbalanced in that the characters must suffer through several chase scenes instead of moving the story along in solving the mystery of the missing scientist or showing the growing attraction between the man and the woman. The story suffers from this sort of glossing over.)** The story then becomes a romance as they spend most of their time making love in a cave. **(The last line in this paragraph shows that the accent of the story has changed from time-travel adventure to time-travel romance—or erotica, depending on how explicit the love scenes are. This is something the reviewer should mention, so a reader who does not like erotica does not wind up with that type of story. It also alerts erotica readers that this is a possible story to interest them. It is up to a reviewer to know the level of sensuality and difference among the subgenres in the various areas of reading.)**

Author (author's name) has constructed a tale about two
people caught up with their emotions and mutual attraction,
but have forgotten their purpose for being in this place. **(Try
to mention the author's name at least once in a short review,
even if the book is not recommended.)** The story begins with
time travel to a dangerous time period, but seems to forget the
dangers as the characters fall into lust. The love scenes occupy
most of the middle and latter thirds of the book to leave the
reader wondering, where is the villain, where is the missing scientist and so forth. The ending is too short and too abrupt. **(This
paragraph shows a breakdown in the plot and why the book
is not recommended by the reviewer. If the book deserves it,
include some positive remarks like, "I found the description exciting and the action scenes well written" and perhaps give an
example of each.)**

Time-travel romance readers may find the story of interest.
This reader felt the author has a premise for a good story, but
it seems like parts of two books were used and not properly
joined. **(This paragraph would be the recommendation or not,
depending on how negatively the reviewer feels about the book.
However, it should be stated as tactfully as possible.)**

Reviewed by (Reviewer's name)

Now let's take a look at what the final review would read
like:

This is a tale about scientists who travel back in time to the
days of dinosaurs to conduct studies of that period. It might appeal to readers who like lots of description to flavor the story or
those who don't mind a slower-paced tale.

The scientists' study is put on hold as the storyline changes to
a search for a missing scientist who preceded them in travel to
this time and place. After wandering through caves and a hidden

valley, they are chased by a variety of dinosaurs. Then, the storyline changes focus to renewing the search for the missing man again.

Flesh-eating monsters are introduced throughout the story to add excitement and a sense of danger. This forces the characters to keep moving, seeking places of safety instead of following the original plotline. The female character slips and falls, winding up with a sprained ankle, thus proving she is a token female. This provides the hero the chance for romantic scenes and he gives several speeches on how he'll get them to safety in true he-man style. Here the time-travel adventure becomes a time-travel romance with erotic scenes.

Author Samuel D. Smith has constructed a tale about two main characters caught up in their emotions and mutual attraction, but have forgotten their purpose for being in this place. The story begins as time travel to a dangerous time period, but seems to forget the dangers as the characters fall into lust. The love scenes occupy most of the middle and latter sections, leaving the reader to wonder who the villain is or what happened to the missing scientist. The ending is too abrupt also.

I did find the description of settings enjoyable and the dinosaurs fearsome. They give the reader a good sense of time and place.

Time-travel romance readers may find this story of interest. This reader felt the author has a good premise for a good story, but it seems like parts of two books were used and not properly joined.

Reviewed by Anne K. Edwards

The middle ground between these two reviews would show the book as readable, but not highly recommended, perhaps just giving it a recommendation for readers who enjoy adventure, or time travel. Also, there are the two extremes that go beyond the limits of these two examples. The first gives too much praise, perhaps using gushing wording or too much enthusiasm, for a good book that isn't really that great. This might be because the reviewer knows the author or has a mistaken idea of a positive review. On the lower extreme is the review that attacks the integrity of the book or author without justification. Such reviews are often written by a person who either enjoys writing overly-negative reviews and the privilege of seeing them in print on sites like Amazon where they are generally removed. Or, such reviews can be written by a reviewer who is either an author or wants to be an author and they allow jealousy of any writer who accomplishes the writing of a book to color their reviews. Reviewers of the extremes have forgotten that objectivity and honesty are required traits for a good reviewer. In writing either gushy or too negative a review, they impugn their own integrity. Authors and readers will soon steer clear of them and any reviews they write will be for their own satisfaction as no one will take them seriously.

Let's take a look at examples of these 'extreme' reviews:

The Sugar-Coated, Overly-Positive, Amateurish Review

Hey, time-travel and adventure fans. This is a great story that you will absolutely love as I did. This is a book that will also appeal to every reader.

If you like the outdoors, and treks into the wilds, then put on your hiking boots, grab up your backpack and join the fascinating characters Harry Dean, Tommy James, Saul Moberg, and Marie Kareen for a jaunt into the back country of Wiscosicos Island off the coast of Maine and back into a time when dinosaurs roamed the Earth.

This very-talented author gives wonderful descriptions of the lush growth and marvelous variety of wildlife found on the island in the days of dinosaurs. I felt like I was there.

The time travelers, led by Harry Dean who really knows his stuff, find this is more than just a scientific trip to study early life forms. They discover their orders also include the fascinating mystery of searching for traces of a paleobotanist who came to this same time and place and never returned. The wonderful writing of Samuel D. Smith quickly carries us to the heart of the matter. I simply couldn't put the book down as Harry Dean split them into two pairs, assigning Marie Kareen to search with Tommy James while he and Saul Moberg investigated some caves they'd found.

The tension was unbearable as they separated only to soon hear Marie screaming. Harry and Saul rush to where they find her standing over the mangled and bloody body of Tommy James. I found the description so vivid that I had to take a deep breath to continue. You can just feel the fear and sorrow the characters have.

It is some time before they can make sense of the mysterious warning she keeps repeating. Convinced a dinosaur attacked Tommy and Marie's words are meaningless, the two men decide to take her with them and resume their search for the missing scientist. You'll just have to know who he is and what happened and the very creative author will keep you in suspense until the end.

Author Samuel D. Smith shows us what the Earth must have been like back then. He makes the Earth tremble under our feet as volcanoes and hot geysers erupt. We'll smell the sulphur and feel the ash trickle down upon us as we hide with Harry's party from marauding dinosaurs. His descriptions are so vivid, you can really see the scenes. The tension is almost unbearable. Mr. Smith made my heart beat really fast and I could scarcely breathe as I read. I kept wanting to know who among the travelers was trying to keep the party from doing its job. Why? This is a fast-moving and action-packed tale that will have you looking for other books by this really great author.

I just loved this book and am sure you will too! I think anyone with a sense of adventure, any time-travel fan who loves stories set in this time, or any reader who just loves suspense and mystery will really enjoy this story. This is surely destined to become a classic. I highly recommend this book. Samuel D. Smith is a really great writer and weaves a story better than most writers I've read.

Reviewed by Anne K. Edwards

The Nasty, Overly-Negative, Amateurish Review

This has to be one of the worst books I ever read. It's supposed to be about time travel and adventure, but mostly the author just tells the reader what he thinks the bugs and volcanoes must have looked like in the days of dinosaurs. The first six pages are about steamy volcanic vents and then the description of a tyrannosaurus rex. I kept wondering where the people were.

The description is unrealistic and stuck in the pages in blocks like you're walking down the street and see a guy get run over, but stop to tell how the clothes he was wearing look. The author doesn't get into the story until page 24 when he just happens to mention the four travelers are looking for a missing paleobotanist who came here before them and was never heard from again. Personally, I thought a dinosaur got him.

Then one of the party is killed, but nobody seems to really care. I guess the author felt he had too many people so he got rid of one of them. He kept the girl, I think, in case he wanted to write in some kind of romance, but it didn't work that way. Instead, the characters wander around some caves, find a hidden valley, and keep hunting for this missing scientist. They never find out what killed the other member of their party. In fact, he's never mentioned again.

The author doesn't know how to describe people and the dialogue is childish at best. I hope he doesn't write any more books until he learns how. There's no plot that I could find and the ending is very abrupt. I felt very unsatisfied with the whole story and I think I wasted my time on this book.

I don't think this author did any research on the time he was writing about, either. He mentioned maple trees and honeysuckle growing in the woods. I don't think they existed back then.

The characters didn't seem to feel anything when they were being chased by the dinosaurs either. Their dialogue was about how their feet hurt and the girl kept saying she wished she'd worn slacks instead of shorts.

I only read this book because I promised I would. I'd never recommend this book to anyone—not even to an enemy—nor any of her other books. Yes, I discovered that Samuel D. Smith's real name is Ellen Jones and I don't think she should be writing books under this name.

Sign me,
Samuel D. Smith

While these last two sample reviews seem extreme, you'd be surprised at the number of similar reviews amateurs post online. Don't fall prey to this disease. Remember to write your review as you would want a review of your own work written—with honesty, tact and objectivity.

Example of a Long, In-Depth Review and Breakdown

In structure, the long, in-depth review will be basically like the short one, but usually will include quotes and more analytical description and criticism. In-depth reviews usually include discussion of major themes in the story, metaphors, symbolism and allegories, as well as a comparison of the work with the author's other works or similar works by other authors in the same genre. In-depth reviews will look in more detail at the style of the author and the mechanics of writing—dialogue, interior monologues, exposition, voice, and other elements that aren't usually discussed in shorter reviews.

Whereas short reviews usually run between 250 and 450 words, long reviews run between 450 and 800 words or more. When including quotes, it is sometimes required to write down in parentheses the number of the page the quote was taken from at the end of each quote, as in the following example. Quotes must not be chosen at random. On the contrary, they should be key quotes that portray important or especially significant points in the story. In-depth reviews are usually written about serious literary works and seldom about genre novels.

Let's break down a long, in-depth review:

Stillbird
by Sandra Shwayder Sanchez
The Wessex Collective
http://www.wessexcollective.com
ISBN: 0-9766274-1-8
Copyright 2005
Trade Paperback, 124 pages, $9.50
Literary

Reviewed by Mayra Calvani

Stillbird is a strangely powerful novel whose haunting, almost surreal images, lyrical, dream-like prose and complexity will challenge the most sophisticated reader. **(The lead is usually more serious than the playful hook of a light review and states some of the qualities of the book, as well as its appropriate audience. From the start the reader knows this is not a story for everybody. The tone of the review sets the tone for the book, and vice versa.)**

Divided into three parts, with each part focusing on a specific character or characters, the novel encompasses different locations and timelines. Either directly or indirectly, the characters and their fates are darkly connected to one another. In a bizarre way the events of the story seem to spring from the strangulation of a midwife who was suspected of witchcraft on the Isle of Skye in the 1880s, and culminate tragically in Denver in the 1960s. **(This paragraph describes the way the book is structured, its setting, and hints at the book's dark tone.)**

In Part One, the reader encounters a lovely Indian woman named Stillbird, a name she gave herself. "She nestled into the leaves and slept soundly without dreaming," writes Sanchez, "but sometimes she woke and watched the stars, and when she woke, it seemed the birds did too, and they spoke to her, and she got her name that night." (15) Before this, she called herself No-Name. Later, she is referred to as "that woman." In fact, Stillbird is "an empty vessel, waiting for the gift of soul and identity." (14) A young widow, Stillbird has to deal with her brother-in-law, Abel, whose obsessive love for her impels him to rape her. **(Some description of Part One, including quotes and some of the plot.)**

With a keen understanding of human motivations, Sanchez offers the reader a chilly portrayal of the twisted psychology of love. Layer by layer, she strips her characters raw. **(Hint that the novel is strong in characterization and that the author does it well and why.)** Abel worships Stillbid, but, ignited by her serene indifference, his love gradually turns to violence. One evening, after an incident involving their son, Abel, for the first time, slaps her hard on the face and discovers something with catastrophic consequences. "He made a formal apology to his wife, after which he made love to her, and she was too confused to deny him. He sensed her confusion as fear, which made him first sad and then satisfied: if she could not love him, let her fear him, he would settle for that." (29) **(Key quote to support the storyline and theme of the story. Note: if the reviewer changes anything in the quoted parts, it is not put in quotes because the change makes it a reworded piece instead, but it still requires the page number the reviewer is paraphrasing from.)**

In Part Two, the reader meets John Banks, an odd figure with a preacher's collar, suede Indian-like boots and "a wide-brimmed hat that looked like he'd gotten it from a theatre's costume room." (53) Full of pathos and hopelessness, he is almost a comical character as he roams from town to town preaching and telling "crazy" stories about the Second Coming. No one takes him seriously, especially when he raves about miracles and how he saved a young girl who was pregnant with the Son of God. Only this baby who comes out of her, this so-called "Jesus," is born with no arms and deemed as a devil. **(Discussion of the main character in Part Two, including some description and quote, as well as a short analytical conclusion of what he represents.)**

In Part Three, Sanchez offers us a disturbing portrayal of Mary, Queen of Scots. A victim of incest, and mother of her father's child, Mary is all that is tragic and painful in the world, a symbol of innocence lost and dreams crushed forever. Her father, seeing her pregnant with his own child, goes to a cave to "ask for a dream to guide him" (97) and decides to kill her. "He held her close to him as he walked in long strides, stepping over rocks and small ravines and snakes that wound, sluggish with cold, toward their winter holes...he lovingly lay her on the ground in a thicket of wild mint, and he took out a knife that he had sharpened so he could not cause her pain, and he carefully cut her throat, feeling a magical strength and sureness in his cold benumbed hands. Carefully, he held her lovely head and carefully, he made the cut." (97) **(A little of the plot in Part Three, discussion of its main character and what she stands for, symbolism, key quotes.)**

Sanchez utilizes the author-omniscient point of view and very little dialogue. The cave is a recurrent image in the novel, and the wild animals add a delicate touch of myth and magical realism. "Once, in mid-summer, when she [Stillbird] fell asleep in the warm afternoon sun in a field of tall grass, and Charles wandered very near to her, the crows all flocked to her and landed on her body, dozens of them, to hide her sleeping form from the man." (40) **(Discussion of author's point of view and symbolism in the novel, more quotes.)**

Sanchez's writing style, though, is exquisite. Her flawless prose flows like "the blood that streamed down her hands [Mary's] and arms as her father carried her to the river that would be her grave." (97) **(Praise for the author's style, supported by quote.)**

Sometimes beautiful, sometimes disturbing, but always memorable, *Stillbird* is a novel I highly recommend for the serious reader. **(Praise. Recommendation and to whom it is recommended. By the end of the review the reader will get a feel for the book based on the quotes, realizing that the evocative writing itself and the symbolism are what make this work stand out.)**

*This review was originally published in *The Bloomsbury Review* (http://www.bloomsburyreview.com). Vol. 26, Issue 1, Jan-Feb 2006

The Article-Review and Breakdown

An article-review usually runs 800 to 1,500 words or more. What sets the article-review apart is that the book is not the only subject discussed in the piece, but some other related subject as well. For example, an article-review could discuss something specific about science fiction or the state of science-fiction literature in general together with a book or books that well exemplify the point the reviewer is trying to make. It usually

includes quotes for better illustrating points and to support the
reviewer's opinion or stance on the subject.

In the following article-review, about 1,000 words, the reviewer discusses the place of new wave fabulist fiction in literature and at the same time reviews an anthology of short stories
that well illustrate her point. An article-review may start as only
a book review and later develop into an article, or vice versa.

Let's look at the example:

*Paraspheres: Extending Beyond the Spheres of Literary and
Genre Fiction*
Edited by Rusty Morrison and Ken Keegan
Omnidawn Publishing
http://www.omnidawn.com
ISBN: 1-890650-18-8
Copyright 2006
Release date: August 2006 (Notice that a pre-publication review
must include the release date.)
Trade Paperback, $19.95, 640 pages
Anthology/New Wave Fabulist Fiction

In the United States, most published fiction falls under two
categories: "genre fiction" and "literary fiction." **(Straight-forward
beginning which states the premise for the article.)**

According to Ken Keegan, editor at Omnidawn Publishing,
genre fiction, which accounts for about 90% of all fiction published, is often defined as "escapist," usually follows a "winning"
formula, and seldom has any lasting literary value. Literary fiction (also referred to as narrative fiction), which accounts for
the remaining 10% of all fiction published, is primarily realistic
and possesses more depth, characterization and lasting cultural
impact. (625-8) **(Credible source to support your argument,
some helpful and informative statistics, paraphrased quotes,
page numbers from which the quotes were taken.)**

But what happens to fiction that doesn't fit into one of these categories? Novels like *The Mists of Avalon, Brave New World,* or *Life of Pi,* for instance—works that have unrealistic settings or plots and aren't officially "literary," yet have incredible depth and power? **(Main question brought up by the article. Puts the question to the reader.)**

As we all know, necessity is the mother of invention. Thus, in the Fall 2002 issue of *Conjunctions,* the literary journal from Bart College, a new term was coined: New Wave Fabulist. Put simply, New Wave Fabulist is non-realistic, literary fiction. You may also think of it as literary fiction with strong elements of horror, science fiction or fantasy. **(Background and historical information.)**

Looking back, other terms have been used to describe this type of fiction: magic realism and speculative. Yet magic realism is chiefly associated with Latin American novelists like Gabriel Garcia Marquez, whose *One Hundred Years of Solitude* greatly exemplifies it. On the other hand, speculative fiction disregards literary quality, making it impossible to always represent serious works. **(More explanatory, historical information and facts.)**

Omnidawn's latest anthology, *Paraspheres: Extending Beyond the Spheres of Literary and Genre Fiction,* excellently illustrates New Wave Fabulist fiction.

The carefully crafted stories, fifty in all, combine elements of magic realism, the paranormal, science fiction, fantasy, mythology, fable, dream vision, even fairy tale, yet are serious literary works filled with symbolism and allegorical power, inviting the reader to ponder at their underlying meaning. **(Note that the first five paragraphs are devoted to the subject of the article. With this paragraph number six, the reviewer finally brings up the book, stating the type of stories the anthology includes.)**

The authors, many who have won prestigious prizes such as the Nebula, Hugo, Kafka, and National Book Awards, and who have published works in such renowned publications as

Ploughshares, Chicago Review, The American Life, The Literary Review, Pearl, Pleiades, The Berkeley Fiction Review, American Literary Review and *Glimmer Train,* among others, offer the reader an interesting array of styles, plots, settings and character studies. **(Some information about the book's authors and awards they have won.)**

In "Skunk," by Justin Courter, the reader takes a mesmerizing glimpse into the mind of a man who has a skunk fetish. "The first time I took skunk musk straight, the effects were overwhelming. I held Homer over my head, squeezed a full shot straight down my throat, and was aware of a burning sensation in my sinuses for an instant before I blacked out. I awoke on the ground, with little idea of how much time had passed. By overdosing the first few times I drank musk, I missed out on much of the experience. Measuring my dosage, I found I could administer myself just enough to induce a sense of euphoria without passing out. Instead of squeezing a full shot directly down my throat, I squeezed Homer over a glass and then used an eyedropper to obtain a single droplet I let fall on my tongue." (421) Needless to say, the story stands as a metaphor for the protagonist's dark childhood. **(Key quote taken from one of the stories to illustrate metaphors used.)**

Contrasting with this morbidity is "The Tree," by Noelle Sickels, which begins as a sweet fairy tale: "Long ago, in a land very far from here, there lived a prince and princess. They had a comfortable castle, which, by magic, stayed clean and in good repair." (382) Not necessarily what you would call a beginning for a serious work of fiction, except this story turns out to be a serious allegory with a powerful message about gender roles. **(Another quote from a very different story to support the reviewer's statement that the book is versatile. The mention of this story further substantiates the sentence written earlier about the stories possessing allegorical power.)**

Stories like "The Ice-Cream Vendor," by Leena Krohn, have strong elements of science fiction in them, while others like "Third Initiation: A Gift From the Land of Dreams" by Mary Mackey, combine dream vision and myth. **(More examples to indicate the versatile quality of the book.)**

"The Town News," also by Justin Courter, tells the paranormal story of a young man who is cursed with the "gift" of being able to visualize people's future deaths as soon as he meets them. Poignant, beautifully written and filled with emotional intensity, this is one of the best stories in the anthology. **(More praise for the stories.)**

Many unforgettable images fill the pages of this book. The following is from "The Secret Paths of Rajan Khanna," by Jeff Vandermeer. Notice how the language flows to create this haunting visual image: "...Rajan notices the boy off to the side, thrown clear, probably a pedestrian, and the way he sits under a newly-planted tree, as if broken in on himself, a blotch of blood spreading across his side, and at first all Rajan can focus on is the spray of blood across the scattered snow, and the way the red, under the lights, doesn't deepen but diffuses as it widens, until it's pink and crystallized in the cold, and then just a shade deeper than the white." (476) **(Quote which supports both the 'strong images' and the 'beauty of the language.')**

In spite of the subject versatility among the stories, one thing ties them together—their authors' faithfulness to the craft and a sharp, fresh imagination. **(Keen observation about the stories— what ties them together in spite of their many differences.)**

At the end of the book, Ken Keegan includes an intriguing and fascinating essay about New Wave Fabulist Fiction—its origins, history, and hopeful future. **(Offers information about other aspects of the book besides the fiction stories.)**

Though the term is controversial, and most scholars will never accept a Fantasy or Science Fiction novel—no matter its depth or sociological impact—as "real" literature, one thing is for sure:

New Wave Fabulist Fiction is a strong force to be reckoned with. **(Conclusion about New-Wave-Fabulist-Fiction drawn by reviewer.)** Most importantly, it is a necessity for those gifted, consummate authors out there who give as much importance to the imagination as they give to the depth of thought and beauty of language. **(Further conclusion which has been substantiated by examples and quotes mentioned above.)**

Reviewed by Mayra Calvani

*This article originally appeared in The Bloomsbury Review (http://www.bloomsburyreview.com). Sept-Oct. 2006

Nonfiction Review

Depending on the publisher or site, word count and depth of review will vary. Some prefer a certain point of view, i.e., faults or flaws in research or references to be pointed out, for example. Some prefer a critique based on a point-by-point reading.

Begin your review as you would begin your fiction review, with:

Title:
Author(s):
Publisher:
Contact Information: (if required)
Copyright:
ISBN:
Format: (if required, page count and price as well)
Genre:

In reviewing any nonfiction or technical work, you need some authority or foundation in the field to produce a well-thought-out, well-written review. In reviewing research papers or similar works, you cannot bluff your way through a reading of the work as experts and other readers would quickly see your errors and reject your review. It would never see publication.

The depth of the review will depend somewhat on the depth of the work to be reviewed. Some are very superficial such as introducing a layman to a particular field, while others will venture into completely unknown regions of that same field. Again, the reviewer must be thoroughly familiar with the area of the work involved. Example: An English professor would not review a paper or book on nuclear physics or architecture. He would review papers related to literature which could encompass basic writing and teaching formats to the most complex interpretations of a very ancient text such as early English folktales.

You will not be writing a critique of the paper, but should assure the audience for which the paper is intended, that the author does know his subject, has done his research and has reached a logical conclusion. Your job as reviewer is not to double-check his research, references or examples, but you should determine if the resulting work is written so anyone in the field will find it readable and of value.

Is the work put forth in an interesting manner so the readers will not fall asleep while trying to wade through it? Does the writer have a command of terminology in the field? Are those terms spelled correctly or will they cause the reader to stop and reach for the dictionary? Does the writing flow well or is it abrupt and hard to follow?

Answering these questions alerts the reader that the paper has been edited and should be an easy read.

Does the author present his points logically or are they written in obtuse language that can confuse the reader into drawing wrong conclusions about the work?

Does the author use references well and logically, perhaps quoting enough to prove he has read the material and knows his field? Does the author build his evidence or present his results in a logical manner that leaves no doubt as to the method of research and its conclusions?

Did the author present anything new in the writing of his book or is it merely a rehash of old factors? For instance, if this is a book with a theory that cannot be proven, does the order of evidence offer a positive support for his conclusions? Are his conclusions arrived at logically and do they support the intent of the book?

Is the book worth reading? Will it add to the sum total of knowledge in this field, or at least, offer a new idea that opens new fields for speculation? An example would be if the writer opens the book with a statement of intent to prove or offer a possible explanation for the origin of the species—man. Has he referred to other writings, listed them, using them for a foundation to build his own theory, to make it seem comprehensible or believable? Or has he just written a lot of words taken from these books without really saying anything new?

When you write your review, state how the overall book is put together, how it is written, and how readable it is. Use quotes to back up any positive or negative statements you make.

A general format would be the hook, a line or two to catch the reader's interest. Then state the intent of the book and whether the writer is successful in putting it forth. Proceed with how the book strikes you, using quotes and perhaps references to support your statements. Then lastly, a summation as to whether the author has attained his goal stated in the beginning, and your recommendation.

Remember, objectivity and honesty in reviewing are of the utmost importance. You are talking to a select audience of readers who depend on your observations for their reading. Do not break the trust or you'll lose your audience.

Following is an example of a short, light review of a non-fiction book aimed at the serious, educated reader interested in psychology.

Exuberance: The Passion for Life
By Kay Redfield Jamison
Vintage Books
ISBN: 0-375-70148-6
Copyright 2005
Paperback, 405 pages, $14.95
Non-Fiction/Psychology

Reviewed by Mayra Calvani

Albert Einstein had it. Teddy Roosevelt had it. Even Mary Poppins and Snoopy had it. **(Interesting lead to grab the reader.)**

Have you ever wondered what exuberance is, and why so many gifted or highly-successful people have it? Is exuberance only seen in humans, or also in animals? Can it be measured? If exuberance is a "passion for life," why is it linked to depression and suicide? Is exuberance an inheritable trait, or a contagious mood? **(This will give the reader a clear idea of the type of questions that are answered in the book.)**

Author Kay Redfield Jamison, Professor of Psychiatry at Johns Hopkins University School of Medicine, answers these questions and more in this brilliant work which explores the essence of exuberance at its core. **(Mention of the author, her qualifications, praise for the book and definition of what it does—all in one sentence.)**

"Exuberance is a psychological state characterized by high mood and high energy," writes Jamison. "...its origins come from the natural world, where its meaning centers on abundance, liveliness, and fertility. It is a more physically alert and active state than joy and of longer duration than ecstasy." **(Quotes are not only for long, in-depth reviews. Here the quote adds a 'spark' to the review and states an interesting fact.)**

According to the author, exuberant people are usually accused of being ridiculous, yet exuberance plays an essential role
in creativity and leadership. What's more, exuberance may very
well play a part in the survival of the species itself because exuberant people are usually energetic, enthusiastic, optimistic and
socially outgoing, traits which increase their attractiveness to
the opposite sex. Yet, exuberance has a dark, dangerous side. In
fact, too much of it can lead to madness. **(Mention of some of
the topics discussed in the book. The last two sentences in this
paragraph hook the reader into wanting to know more about
the subject.)**

Jamison investigates exuberance as seen throughout the ages
and within different contexts like the animal world, literature,
music, art, science, politics and religion. She takes famous people
and characters and uses them as examples, using many quotes
and references from famous sources. **(Some information on how
the author has written the book and done research.)**

The book is filled with fascinating facts and insights about the
human mind, and was clearly researched extensively **(supported
by the sentence in the earlier paragraph which states that the
author used many quotes and references)**. Though Jamison
writes with surprising grace and enthusiasm, this work is still
a heavy read, but one which will be relished by serious readers
of psychology. Highly recommended. **(Mention of the author's
style, as well as the audience intended for the book. Level of
recommendation.)**

Reviewed by Mayra Calvani

*This review originally appeared in *Armchair Interviews*
(http://www.armchairinterviews.com).

In order to turn this review into a long, in-depth one, you'd
need to add more critical analysis, more quotes, and perhaps

discuss comparisons with other similar books in the field.

A negative review of this book would have lacked the interesting lead and positive words and comments. Possible reasons for not recommending this book would have been obvious lack of research by the author, typos and grammatical mistakes, redundancies of either words or ideas or both, an inability by the author to fully prove or demonstrate her point or make her ideas clear, or any of the various reasons pointed out earlier in this section. You should support your negative statements with reasons or examples. Positive elements about the book should be pointed out too, even if few.

The Children's Book Review and Breakdown

Children's book reviews are usually shorter and lighter. They usually run between 150-250 words. In the case of picture books, you must add the name of the photographer or illustrator under the author's name. You must also specify the age group the book is addressing. In the body of the review, it is helpful to state the moral message of the story. Remember that with young children's books, it is usually the parent who will choose or approve it. Also, the reviewer must make an assessment of the illustrations and how they compliment the story. Maybe the story is fine but the illustrations are ugly or scary. Maybe the pictures are beautiful and evoking but the story is flat. It is the job of the reviewer to let the reader know how the writing and illustrations compliment each other. Also, a reviewer must make a special assessment of the language in the case of rhyming story books.

As with other types of reviews, if the book (or author/illustrator) has won an award, it should be mentioned, too.

Let's look at the positive review below:

Baby Dog Beans Comes Home: A Paul and Beans Adventure by
Jennie Hale Book
Photos by Jennie Hale Book
Abbott Avenue Press
http://www.AbbottAvenuePress.com
ISBN: 0-9767514-2-9
Copyright 2005
Hardcover, 24 pages, $13.95
Children's, 2 and up

What is it about golden retrievers that makes a dog lover,
young or old, go wild? **(The hook may start with a question.)**

In *Baby Dog Beans Comes Home*, author Jennie Hale Book
captures the sweet "magic" of these gentle, devoted, intelligent
dogs while offering young children an important message with
which they can identify. **(What the author has accomplished
with the story. What the story offers the reader.)**

The story is seen from the perspective of Paul, the older dog
who until now has been the only "child" in the family, and Beans,
the new baby brother. More than anything, Beans wishes to be
accepted by his older brother, but Paul is not ready to be friends,
play catch, or share any of his toys. As a matter of fact, Paul
liked it a lot better when it was just him. All this changes when
Beans runs into serious trouble and Paul rescues him. **(Some of
the plot.)**

As Paul realizes in the end, "It's not always easy when a new
brother or sister comes into the family. But even if you're not best
friends right away...give them a chance and you'll have someone
who'll be there for you your whole life. And that's pretty great."
**(Quote may be added to the review. Here the theme or moral
message of the story becomes clear, helpful if the parent is spe-
cifically looking for a book about sibling rivalry.)**

This is a book that can be read to a very young child, and
one that early readers will relish on their own. The large,

adorable photographs are sure to delight people of all ages. (Recommendation. States the preferred audience for the book, as well as a positive comment about the pictures.)

Reviewed by Mayra Calvani

*This review originally appeared in *The Bloomsbury Review* (http://www.bloomsburyreview.com). March/April 2006.

Again, a negative review version of this book would have lacked the intriguing, enthusiastic lead, and might point out an inability by the author to bring her message across or catch the gentleness of these dogs. If the photos used in the book were unprofessionally taken, blurry, or even scary (contradicting the purpose of the story), this should also be discussed in the evaluation.

The Anthology Review and Breakdown

For anthology reviews, whether or not they're literary or commercial, you will follow the same guidelines as with novels. The only difference is that, in this case, you will state a little of the plot of each—or some—stories in the anthology. You may choose the stories you think are particularly more intiguing or better plotted, the choice is up to you. If there are inconsistencies (maybe some stories are excellent and some mediocre), be sure to let the reader know.

As with other books, reviews for this type of fiction may be short and light, or long and in-depth. Following is an example of a positive anthology review. At about 550 words, this falls on the lower edge of a long review. Deleting the long quote would make it qualify for a short review. To make it longer, a closer look at some of the individual stories would be necessary.

Unkempt
By Courtney Eldridge
Harcourt
ISBN: 0-15-603208-2
Copyright 2004
Trade Paperback, 262 pages, $14.00
Fiction/Literary Anthology

Reviewed by Mayra Calvani

4 ½ stars (*Curled Up With A Good Book* rating)

In this original, brilliant collection of short stories, New
Yorker Courtney Eldridge offers us a twisted, askew glimpse
into the darkest corners of the human mind and the fears of
our present society. Eldridge does this with a razor-sharp eye,
candidness, and a wacky sense of humor. **(Rave lead, letting the
reader know immediately the tone of the review; states what
the author offers the reader and how she achieves this.)**

Unkempt has seven stories and one novella, and presents an
array of desperate and pathetic characters who either are trying
to cope with the helplessness of their lives, or are completely
and painfully unaware of it: a blocked writer who systemati-
cally erases everything she writes, a woman who thinks there
are sharks in regular swimming pools, a lady who is unaware she
has obsessive-compulsive disorder, a clerk at a retail store who is
accosted by demented customers, an alcoholic mother who can't
understand her daughter's behavior, an ex-porn star who now is
trying to keep her first "real" relationship afloat—these are some
of the characters you'll meet in this darkly hilarious anthology.
**(General description of the anthology, tempting the reader
with an intriguing array of characters and offering glimpses into
what the stories are about, states the tone of the writing.)**

The author's writing style can be quite smothering at times, as no quotation marks or new paragraphs are used to separate dialogue. It is a clever techique to impart the same feelings of "confusion" and "desperation" to the reader as the character is feeling. **(Mentions an unusual technique employed by the author and what it achieves.)** That said, Eldridge's writing is incredibly revealing and illuminating. In fact, the ability to combine these two aspects is Eldridge's gift. The following passage, taken from "Sharks," perfectly exemplifies the writing style used throughout the book:

"You honestly believe there are sharks at the Sol Goldman Y? I asked. It's not about believing, it's about my fear. This is my fear I'm talking about. I got that much, I said. Well, there you go, she said. You asked, I told you. No, you're right, okay. But tell me this, what happens if you get into a swimming pool? I asked. I don't unless I have to, she said. But if you went to a pool, wouldn't you be able to see the sharks, swimming around in the pool? I mean, wouldn't *somebody* notice that there was a shark in the pool? Or do they have a cloaking device, too? Very funny, she says, but the answer is no. No, you wouldn't necessarily see them. They just wait, she said. You mean the sharks wait somewhere in the pool? I asked, clarifying again. Yes, she said. Where? Where would they wait, the drain? I don't know where they might be waiting, see, *that's the thing*. They could be waiting anywhere. Of course, I said." **(Key quote to support the statement about the author's style/technique mentioned in the previous paragraph.)**

Some passages, like the one above, made this reviewer laugh out loud. Yet the message is undeniably troubling, people live in irrational fear these days, and this specific story can very well serve as an allegory for the present state of terrorism. **(Mention of symbolism/allegories in the collection.)** Though Eldridge's style is different in many ways, it is in some aspects similar to

Tama Janowitz's. Certainly both combine the sharp eye, dark hilarity, and askew angles of probing into the deepest corners of the human mind. **(Here the author's work is compared to another author who writes in the same genre, and why.)** If there's only one negative comment to say about this collection, that would have to be a certain lack of versatility. The stories are original, but the "voice" behind all of them at times sounds the same. **(States the negative aspect of the book—and the reason the reviewer gave 4 ½ stars instead of 5.)** However, this doesn't take away the fact that *Unkempt* is an intriguing, fascinating anthology, one this reviewer is very glad to have read. **(Conclusion and recommendation; it's important to let the reader know how a book can be excellent in spite of one negative element.)**

*This review was originally published in *Curled Up With A Good Book* (http://www.curledup.com).

To turn this positive review into a negative review, your lead would have to reflect the tone of your evaluation or be neutral and state facts. You would have to offer a brief description of the anthology as a whole and then of several of the stories. In the review above, the author has purposely chosen a 'smothering' style as a clever technique to bring her message across. If this were not the case and the author had simply been obtuse, then you would have to support this with an example(s). Most often, the trouble with anthologies is either that the stories are flat and boring, or that they lack versatility and sound the same. Using the guidelines discussed in earlier sections of this book, you would have to make an intelligent, fair assessment as to why the book doesn't live up to its full potential.

The Difference between Reader
Reviews and Reviewer Reviews

Reader reviews can be of any length, have no set pattern, go overboard with praise or negative remarks, inadvertently give away the ending, and say things a reviewer wouldn't. There are no rules or guidelines for reader reviews, giving a reader the freedom to write whatever they wish in whatever style they wish.

This is not to say that a reader review may not be well written, that the reader's opinion is not well expressed, or that it doesn't have merit, only that it doesn't follow the structure or organization of a review written by a reviewer who has had to learn the requirements of many sites or publications for whom they write.

A reader who enjoys writing reviews may graduate into becoming a reviewer. On doing this, the differences will become obvious between the two types of reviews as they deliberate on how to present a review that will reflect well on themselves as well as the site publishing it. The freedom of expression becomes somewhat limited and a reader moving into serious reviewing will learn self-control is their greatest asset.

The reviewer must be objective and fair in their comments, whether or not the book is one they would read for pleasure. A reviewer works hard to build a reputation for honesty and integrity and must carefully consider what they write to maintain that reputation. This is something a reader writing reviews does not need to consider and this is the basic difference between the two types of reviews.

Having said this, the term 'reader reviews' can be misleading. The reason for this is that many online sites that accept reviews by freelance reviewers do so under their section of 'Reader Reviews', thus you have both readers and freelance reviewers submitting reviews under the same category, with the result that both types of reviews end up mixed together. The most obvious example here would be Amazon, but the same goes for many other online review sites which have their system set up in this manner.

The Difference between Pre-Publication and Post-Publication Reviews

A reviewer may be asked to read an Advance Reading Copy (ARC) of a manuscript before it is printed as a finished product. These requests may take two forms—one is a blurb/endorsement for publicity that may go on the book jacket and/or website when published under the heading of "what people are saying about this book" and the second form is writing a pre-publication review (or a preview).

The pre-publication review is aimed at bringing the pending publication of the book to the attention of libraries, bookstores, and various booksellers' associations whose newsletters spread the word about new books.

Most of the pre-publication reviews are handled by publications such as *Publishers Weekly, Library Journal, School Library Journal, Kirkus, Booklist, New York Times Book Reviews*, and *Foreword Magazine* among others. Most request bound galleys and want them sent four to five months before the release date.

According to an article in *Poets and Writers Magazine*, pre-publication reviews are used by librarians and booksellers to know what books to order and recommend to readers. A title listed in pre-publication review journals has a better chance of getting coverage from some newspapers and magazines. Also, a pre-publication review in one of these publications may (though not always) guarantee over a thousand sales to libraries/bookstores.

While the pre-publication review informs those who order multiple copies, the post-publication review is aimed at the individual reader and some retailers. The best use of this review is at the time of release or just after release in order to garner attention for new books.

With thousands of books being published annually, the reader who uses reviews to help decide on purchasing or not purchasing a book prefers to do so when the book is new. Any review is quickly buried under newer ones and as quickly forgotten. Some authors use a system of getting more reviews to keep the book in sight of readers. These are generally posted on review websites.

Any reviewer should be aware of these differences so if they are asked to do a pre-publication review of a book instead of a post-publication review, they will keep the use of such in mind.

How a Review Differs from a Book Report,
a Critique and a Press Release

It's easy to confuse reviews with book reports, critiques and press releases until you've written a few. Then the differences will quickly become apparent to reviewers or readers.

A review should contain a little of the plot without giving away any part of the story that makes reading it unnecessary (like the end or the so-called 'spoilers'). This can have unforeseen consequences such as the author suing the reviewer and any site foolish enough to post that review. Any review is a personal opinion based on a reader's reaction to the various components of the story such as characterization, setting, description, plot, pacing, and so on. However, a review also has the consumer and price of the book in mind. People read reviews to help make up their minds about a book, but in the end other factors affect their decision, such as price, the author being known to them, the cover which usually has a large influence on such decisions, and the genre. A well-done review can give a prospective buyer an idea of whether or not a book is worth its cost and the time invested in reading it. Since a review is an individual's opinion, it is subjective (even though, as stated earlier, that reviewers must be objective when writing a review, in the sense that they shouldn't be biased). The ultimate aim of a review is to recommend or not to recommend the book.

A book report is usually written as a requirement to some classroom work and acts as an outline of the total book, including the ending since it is not meant for publication. It examines and judges the book for its own merits. It is objective rather than subjective. The person writing the report summarizes the whole plot. The focus is factual rather than evaluative. (This is the reason why too much focus on story and not enough on evaluation will make a review look like a book report—another sign of an amateur reviewer.) There's no concept of 'spoilers' as

with a review. Since it's not consumer oriented, there's no recommendation—although it may contain the reader's impression
as a conclusion. A book report is written for the book's sake
without the cost of the book or the reader in mind.

Reviews and book reports are written about *published* books.
Critiques, on the other hand, are mostly written for *unpublished*
manuscripts. The aim of a critique is to improve the manuscript
prior to publication and is usually done at the request of the
author. While similar to a review, it is an analytical evaluation.
However, it is much longer, in-depth, detailed, and critical—
pointing out weaknesses the critiquer finds. Like the long, in-
depth review, a critique answers a lot more questions than a
short review does.

A review usually focuses on plot, pacing, characterization,
description and dialogue while a critique examines every aspect of a book such as plot, pacing, characterization (of not only
protagonists but secondary characters as well), description, dialogue, themes, symbolism, allegories, etc. These elements of the
book are examined in detail in the critique and problems found
are set forth with possible ways to fix them suggested. The critiquer judges the book on its own merits.

An important difference between a review and a critique is
that the critiquer must be a writer who is thoroughly conversant
with all aspects of writing while the reviewer may be a reader
who only wants to share their opinion of any book. The critiquer must be professionally qualified in the field of the book
they are critiquing. The end result is that a review summarizes
some part of the plot and the critique dissects the book into its
parts and does not summarize it.

A press release is the least similar to the review. It is an
'announcement' of a book that has been published and just
released. It is news. The aim of a press release is not to make
a recommendation but to attract the media and create 'buzz,'
to promote and publicize the book. A press release is never

negative because it would defeat its purpose. It is not an opinion and contains no evaluation. A press release has its own specific layout, totally different from a review. (For a sample of a press release, see Appendix.) A press release, however, may contain key review quotes in its body in order to tease and hook the media.

Review

- An individual's opinion.
- It is subjective, consumer-oriented with an aim and focus of evaluating/recommending a book.
- It contains a short summary of the plot that doesn't give away the ending—also called a spoiler.
- A review is written only on published books and may be written by readers as well as reviewers.

Book Report

- A book report is objective and not consumer-oriented. It judges the book by its own merits.
- The focus is factual rather than evaluative.
- The book report is a summary of the whole plot including spoilers and ending.
- There's no recommendation (though the conclusion may include the reader's impression of the book).
- The book report is only written on published books and is usually assigned in schools and universities and written by students.

Critique

- A critique is an individual's opinion.
- It is subjective (though not to the extent of a review), is not consumer-oriented, and judges a pre-publication manuscript on its own merits.

- The focus is critical and evaluative.
- It examines and analyzes ALL important elements of a book.
- The aim is to improve the manuscript by pointing out strengths and weaknesses with suggested solutions.
- There's no recommendations to readers, the dialogue is between the author and the critiquer.
- A critique is done on unpublished manuscripts, almost always by a writer or editor with a thorough knowledge of the field.

Press Release

- The press release is an announcement to the media.
- It is media-oriented and never negative.
- It has its own specific layout.
- Its aim is to create buzz and attract the media to the book and its author.
- The press release may contain review quotes in its body and is done for published books only.
- It is usually written by the author, publisher or publicist.

The Difference between Book Reviewing
and Book Criticism

The difference between book reviewing and book criticism—also referred to as literary book criticism or academic reviews—is not often clear and a lot of people confuse these terms. Book reviewing and book criticism share many things in common, but their main distinction lies in their intent.

In book reviewing, the main purpose of the reviewer is to let the reader know whether or not the book is worth buying without spoiling the reading experience. Book criticism, on the other hand, examines the book in much more detail for the work's sake and, generally, with the assumption that the reader has already read the book. This is the reason why, unlike with book reviewing, the idea of giving away spoilers isn't an issue in book criticism.

"Book reviews are primarily about new books and offer an opinion about whether the book is worth purchasing and reading," says Corinne Demas, author and Fiction Editor of *The Massachusetts Review* (http://www.CorinneDemas. com). "Literary criticism is in-depth study of a work of literature for itself, and does not take into consideration its commercial value. It usually concerns books that have already earned a place on library shelves." She also states that "the issue of 'spoilers' doesn't really come up in academic reviews because when you're writing about literature it's never the plot that matters, but the work as a whole. The interest is in the artistry that leads to an ending, not the facts of the ending itself."

Let's take *Madame Bovary* as an example. It's known to most people that this novel has an unhappy ending, but that is not a deterrent for people to go ahead and read the novel. Readers aren't really concerned plot-wise about what's going to happen at the end; what matters to them is the way Flaubert brings the characters to life and the artistry with which he succeeds in making the novel so compelling. Knowing that the protagonist will die doesn't alter the reading experience. People who read book criticism primarily focus on the author's skill and techniques and not on plot. They want to learn the meaning of a book. It's not a surprise why book criticism mostly deals with classics and literary novels.

"Many people are not quite sure what the difference is between a book review and book or literary criticism," says Irene Watson, author and founder of Reader Views (http://www.readerviews.com)."The primary purpose of a book review is to present enough information about the book to help a person decide whether to read it. A review will state what the book is about, without giving away a novel's plot, or the conclusions of an argument in a non-fiction book. Think of a book review as similar to a movie preview. Literary criticism, on the other hand, is written for people who have already read the book and are interested in exploring the meaning behind the work. The literary critic is sharing his or her thoughts, opinions, and interpretation of the work, based on a close reading of the text, with the reader, as if the two are having a conversation about the work. Criticism is like the afterword to a book; it may give away the plot because it assumes the reader has already read the book—that's why, when reading the classics, it's best to read the introduction last, after you form your own opinion of the work."

Book criticism is usually published in print university and literary journals and focuses on serious works of literature and not commercial novels. Unlike the average review, which has a 400-600 word count, book criticism can be as long as 2,000 words.

Book criticism is seldom published online and never on popular review sites, blogs, or online retailers like Amazon. Beware that including spoilers in these sites may even be cause for a lawsuit by the author or publisher.

The Absolute Don'ts (or Signs of an Amateur)

Avoid the following mistakes like you would avoid a hot oven. These mistakes scream AMATEUR!

- Don't give away the ending when talking about the plot, nor give away important plot twists or "spoilers." Knowing the ending of a book without having read it is like knowing the end of a movie without having seen it. And that's no fun!

- Don't leave out the evaluation. You'd be surprised at how many fledgling reviewers out there leave out this important part of a review. A summary or synopsis of the story is not an evaluation. Simply saying "I loved this book, and you will love it too" is not an evaluation. You must clearly explain the reason or reasons why you loved it. Besides, expressions like this one are clichés.

- Don't sugar-coat a review. Using phrases like "This is the best book I've ever read in my life" will raise incredulity and suspicion in the intelligent reader. Facile praise is for ad copies, not reviews. Never be afraid to criticize when you feel you have to. Remember your main duty is to the reader.

- Never be mean, harsh, rude or tactless. You can be critical and honest without being unkind. Instead of saying "This is a terrible book," you can say "I didn't enjoy this book for the following reasons...." or "This book didn't live up to its full potential because...."

- Don't be overly academic or pompous to try to impress readers. The purpose of reviews is not to glorify the reviewer. Reviews are about books and the readers, NOT the reviewer. Even with academic reviews, there's no need to become blindly immersed in the hidden meanings of a book. Be insightful, but never obtuse. "Stanislaw Lem was quoted as saying that the reviews of his book *Solaris* were so profound that he didn't recognize the story anymore," says Ralph Briggs of *Yet Another Book Review Site* (http://www.yetanotherbookreview.com), which focuses on science fiction, fantasy and horror reviews. Don't steal someone else's book and transform it into your own creation!

- Never leave out the book's information (title, publisher, copyright year, ISBN, etc.). This is a must for libraries, bookstores and retailers when ordering books.

- Never submit your review without making sure it is free of spelling, grammatical and punctuation mistakes. A person who doesn't know how to write proper English has no business reviewing books. "A lot of reviewers seem to be more in love with the idea of seeing their own name on screen than they are in making sure that their reviews are well-written and thorough. They don't realize, perhaps, that their material will hang around for years to come, and that one day they might want to review *seriously* for an actual, real magazine or newspaper, and there'll be this huge archive of all their slap-dash, half-assed efforts for potential editors/employers to see," says Ariel, editor of *The UK SF Book News Network* (formerly *The Alien Online*).

The Feelings of an Author

Though a reviewer's first responsibility rests with the reader, this doesn't mean that the author's feelings should be ignored, especially if they're first-time authors. It's interesting to note that many reviewers are 'ruthless' with established authors yet 'give breaks' to first-time authors.

Review publications, both print and online, have various levels of tolerance when it comes to authors' feelings. In general, most print publications consider an author's feelings completely irrelevant, while online review sites tend to be more sympathetic. This is partly the reason—though not the only one—why libraries and booksellers stick to the major review publications and ignore the online sites (this topic will be discussed further in Part II). This is not to say that some online review sites aren't as tough as the print publications. In fact, in response to this double standard, it is safe to say that online review publications are becoming more and more demanding and scrupulous with their reviews.

"Nobody wants to write a mean review," says Barbara Hoffert, Book Review Editor, *Library Journal* (http://www.libraryjournal.com), "and in fact I find a review that is too gleefully negative a little suspect. If a review must be negative, I prefer carefully-documented objections to an endless rant. But in the long run we must be concerned with meeting the needs of our readers, not shielding an author's feelings. That's just not our job."

The secret, of course, is to keep the author's feelings in mind without allowing them to influence the review. A reviewer should be aware of the enormous amount of time and effort that the average author puts into a book while remaining truthful. "You'd have to be pretty lacking in empathy not to take into account all the author has invested, but any book needs to stand on its own—it's been said that manuscripts are authors' babies and that having them rejected, whether by critics, readers, or publishers, is incredibly painful," says Sharon Schulz-Elsing, owner and book review editor at *Curled Up With A Good Book* (http://www.curledup.com). "On the other hand, if you pay a stonemason to build you a retaining wall, you expect the finished product to hold back the dirt, stand up straight, and generally succeed at its purpose. Same goes for a book."

The ironic thing is that no matter how tactful a reviewer is when writing a negative review, some authors are always going to take offense. Taking criticism is always hard. For most authors, it can be difficult to accept that there's something wrong with their work. "Editors and publishers and publicists have feelings," says James Cox, editor-in-chief at *Midwest Book Review* (http://www.midwestbookreview.com). "Someone will always be so sensitive that no matter how diplomatic you are in giving their book a non-recommendable referendum you will not be able to avoid hurting their feelings or bursting their bubble. Just don't go out of your way to be nasty about it."

In the end, all you need to concern yourself with is gathering your thoughts to the best of your ability and writing a well-thought-out, intelligent, honest review. Feeling sorry for the author is not in your 'job' description and won't take you very far as a reviewer.

What if the Book is Terrible?

Sometimes books are so horribly written the best thing to do is refuse to review them. Books filled with punctuation, spelling and grammatical mistakes shouldn't be published in the first place. Usually these badly-written books are self-published or come from subsidy or vanity presses. Some books may be well copyedited but lack all the major elements that make a good book. There's no focus in the story, no plot, stilted dialogue, redundancies, too much telling, stereotyped characters, and endless 'talk' that goes on and on without making any sense. Other times—and this is more common with spiritual memoirs published by subsidy companies—the books carry on and on about situations that couldn't possibly interest anybody on the planet, that are so boring it becomes a torture to keep turning the pages. It is because of this stigma and the foreknowledge that they'll be full of mistakes that many reviewers refuse to review subsidized or vanity-published books. This is the same with presses who claim to be 'traditional' and won't charge the authors to publish their books yet don't do any editing and make their money from selling overpriced copies back to that author.

You don't have to become a masochist to be a reviewer. If you were to write a review of this kind of book, it would be difficult to keep it tactful because it defies tact. The review would end up being so harsh you would actually be doing a favor to the author or publisher by not reviewing it. Besides, there are so many well-written books out there. Why give exposure to badly-done books? Why spend your energy on them?

In this situation, you're not ethically obligated to return the book to the author, though some reviewers choose to do so. There is a 'silent' agreement between the author (or publisher/publicist) and a reviewer if the book is terrible, and the reviewer may choose not to review it.

Reviewing a badly-written book takes more time and effort than most reviewers deem worthwhile. Some reviewers won't review certain presses or certain authors for this reason.

Fortunately, most books you'll receive won't fall into this extreme category.

Is It Unethical to Sell the Book?

While it is not considered 'illegal' for legitimate review-ers to sell the books they've reviewed, there seems to be a big controversy as to whether or not this practice is 'ethical'.

As usual, when one mentions the word 'ethical,' one is opening a can of worms.

From one side of the debate, people find the practice: tacky, cheesy, wrong, unfair, questionable, frowned upon, and synonymous with theft. Their main argument is that books are sent to reviewers as gifts, and to sell these books would be to deny royalties to the authors. These people usually agree it is okay to donate the books to libraries, homes, hospitals, and charity organizations.

From the other side of the debate are those who believe it is the reviewer's right to sell the books if they wish. Their ar-guments are the following:

- Books are not sent to reviewers as gifts, but as an ex-change for their time and effort, and reviewers are free to dispose of them as they wish—sell, donate, or toss them into a bonfire!

- Some reviewers receive hundreds of books a year, more than they can keep. What are they supposed to do with these unwanted books? They must dispose of them somehow.

- If one follows the same logic, donating books also denies authors those royalties, so there's no difference to that author royalty-wise if the books are donated or sold. Moreover, many books donated to libraries end up being resold by these libraries. Authors won't see royalties for these books one way or another. If you go a little further and follow the same logic, what about selling second-hand books? What about second-hand bookstores? Are the authors being compensated here?

- A book resold by a reviewer is a small price to pay for the publicity. Let's face it, reviews are the least expensive and most effective ways to promote a book or an author's name. Ads on online sites and print publications can be ridiculously expensive. Authors and publishers should feel grateful that most reviewers work without charging. What would happen if this were to change? Do you really want to put restrictions on legitimate reviewers?

- A book resold by a reviewer is kept in circulation, providing the author more exposure. In the long run, it opens more possibilities for the author if a review copy is resold to a new reader. This new reader might like the book and check out the author's other works, which might end up in new sales for that author. Believe it or not, some authors have made important connections with Hollywood-studio executives only because a reviewer decided to sell a review copy to make a few bucks.

- For publishers, it is part of their marketing plan to send review copies. Review copies are written off as a marketing 'expense.' Publishers must be prepared to accept that some are going to be resold.

Up to this point we have been talking about review copies that are finished books. But what about printed galleys and ARCs? (A galley is the printed copy of the manuscript in 8 x 11 sheets of paper, printed on one side, and may or may not be bound. An ARC is an advance reading copy, it is a copy of the book that has been set up in the format of the book it will become, but it hasn't been edited or changed.)

While many people believe it is all right for reviewers to sell review copies, almost everyone agrees that this is not the case with galleys and ARCs. Even though authors don't receive royalties on these, and reselling them wouldn't be depriving the authors of a sale, most people agree that this is an unethical practice. The Authors Guild has strong opinions against selling ARCs. The reason is that ARCs are not finished books and they might change from the time they are sent to the reviewer to the time they are officially published to the public. Nevertheless, in spite of the fact that they're usually stamped with NOT FOR SALE, ARC's are commonly sold on sites like eBay, sometimes at exorbitant prices. They can even be found for sale in bookstores! The reason ARCs and galleys seem so attractive, especially if signed, is that they are viewed by readers as collectible items and 'special first prints,' especially if the authors are well known.

In summing up, while galleys and ARCs should not be used beyond the purpose of being read by reviewers, and many review sites and print publications have strict guidelines concerning these, the reality is that reviewers sell them all the time (though they probably won't admit that).

So how can the re-selling of review copies or ARCs be prevented? How about having the authors and publishers add a SASE with the book if they want it back? Is it feasible? It's hard to believe authors and publishers would be willing to take the expense. Returned books would have to be sold as used books and authors and publishers wouldn't get enough to cover the cost of the book, envelope and postage.

As for ebooks, they aren't sold ninety-nine percent of the time because of the difficulty in doing so without advertising you're selling copies of the book and for this you can be prosecuted.

Selling one print copy as used is one thing but selling ebooks is quite another as it would require actually marketing the product to make it worthwhile reselling it. There have been cases where sites, set up as 'clubs,' have been selling ebooks without permission. These sites were quickly put out of business. Most people feel it is not worth the risk of heavy fines and jail time to resell ebooks.

It is the reviewer's right to sell any book they have, but they should honor the agreement of providing a review if they agreed to do so. That fact is, once the copy of the book is delivered into the hands of the reviewer, it becomes their property. Books sent that weren't asked for are also the recipient's property. And one may dispose of one's property one way or another without permission. Donations for resale by libraries are considered a charity and that benefits everyone in the long run.

In the end, it all boils down to whether or not the reviewer is legitimate. The legitimate reviewer's primary goal is not to sell books, but to read books and write reviews. The truth is, most reviewers do what they do because they love reading, not because they want to make a few bucks. If they were after money, the last thing they would be doing is reviewing books! (The exception here is staff reviewers for major newspapers and publications.)

At the lower extreme, you have the people who call themselves reviewers to get books only to turn around and resell the book and never do a review. These people do not even read the books. They are thieves and liars who prey on writers and eventually their names become known and people won't send them any more books. There is a name for what they do, and that is fraud, which is a prosecutable offense. Don't set yourself up as a reviewer that falls into this category. You'd be the loser in the short run.

Ownership and Print Rights

Any reviewer must keep in mind who holds the right to any review they write. It is generally understood that reviews are called an intellectual property and the property of the writer. However, if the reviewer is working as a staff reviewer for a site that claims all rights to a review, they have surrendered their claims to it by taking the position and knowing ahead of time such is the case. If the reviewer does not work for such a site and is independent, the ownership of the review remains to them and they may grant author, publisher, or other sites permission to use it to promote the book so long as they are credited with writing the review.

Review sites such as *Reader to Reader* (http://www. readertoreader.com) and *Curled Up With A Good Book* (http:// www.curledup.com) become the sole owner of reviews done for their sites. To submit these reviews the reviewer, author or publisher must request special permission to use it to promote the book from the review editor or site owner/moderator. Also, publications like *The Bloomsbury Review* (http://www. bloomsburyreview.com) and *Armchair Interviews* (http:// www.armchairinterviews.com) want first print rights and request, if the review is submitted elsewhere, you specify the fact that they originally published the review. Some of these sites and publications do not want the reviews published again for a certain time period which might be a month or more. Here too, it is proper to request the publication's agreement ahead of submitting the review to other sites or publications.

An example of crediting a site or publication with publishing the review originally is:

*This review originally appeared in *The Bloomsbury Review* (or wherever).

Do not assume that any online publication or site that claims rights to a review will not mind if you submit your reviews to other places unless they are a site that welcomes reviews from any review source. Be sure to ask the review editor in advance. Each review publication and site has its own policy about this and it is up to you to learn what it is. A good reviewer will always respect the publication's policies concerning reviews.

When the Hobby Turns into a Demanding Job

For staff reviewers who work for major newspapers and publications, reviewing is a demanding job. They have strict deadlines. They must deal with authors, publishers and publicists pressuring them. They might be instructed to write nasty or praising reviews by their editors. Sometimes they receive hundreds of books in a week, and even though there's no way to review so many books, they must try to review as many as possible. These reviewers have slush piles of unsolicited books that they will never review because of time constraints. Professional reviewers are another way the larger names gain attention for their work so they are a publicity tool in that light. Most of the big-time reviewers require a query first before accepting any book for review unless they have an unwritten contract with the author, publisher or publicist. They are not open to the online author. They do not accept ebook copies. Some want a copy of the finished book and often that book will be sold online somewhere without ever having been reviewed. Many honorable reviewers will tell you up front that they don't have time to review your book, though it is unrealistic to believe that they will answer every query they receive.

For freelance reviewers, especially beginners, reviewing is another story. It usually begins as a fun hobby where the compensation is the book itself, the chance to read an author's work, and the satisfaction of seeing their review published in print or online. It's exciting to receive new books in the mail, even more so if the books are in the reviewer's favorite genre or by their favorite author. Many freelance reviewers also accept ebook copies.

Reviewing can soon become addictive and as you develop a taste for it, your craving for review copies will increase. If you write good reviews, pretty soon review sites and review publications may request more of your work, sometimes to such extent that you'll be loaded with more review copies than you can handle. Indeed, you might wake up one day to realize that what started as a fun, light hobby has suddenly turned into a tough, almost full-time job. Maybe in the beginning it was enough to read leisurely at night, while now meeting review deadlines requires more reading time. Maybe now reviewing is getting in the way of your real job or other important family activities. If you feel stressed out and overwhelmed with books to review, you might be overdoing it, which can have negative consequences because you may find yourself skimming rather than reading and your reviews might feel 'rushed,' or, worse yet, might have mistakes and errors related to the book's plot or characters. It is embarrassing when an author or publisher points out to you that you got the facts wrong or mistook the name of a character.

Though it is well known in the industry that staff reviewers of major newspapers sometimes don't have time to read the books and simply write their reviews based on the promotional material (press release or media kit) accompanying the review copy, there's no ethical reason for a freelance reviewer to do this. This is NOT reviewing in any form. This is merely a promotional trick of the trade and shows laziness on the part of the reviewer and cheats the reader. This is unfair to the person who sent you the book expecting you to write an honest opinion.

One way to avoid this is not to get too carried away when requesting review copies. Be realistic and only request what you can handle. This is not only fair to you but to the author as well. Of course, there's nothing you can do when books you have never requested arrive in the mail. Fortunately, most review sites allow only a maximum number of books to be requested by a reviewer at one specific time. But if you review for several sites, then it is up to you to set your own maximum quota.

Making a name for yourself as a prolific reviewer is fine, but not at the expense of a well-written review. There's nothing wrong with wanting to be the number one reviewer on Amazon, for instance, but if your reviews become 'generic' and begin to sound the same, then maybe you should pause and consider the following: what is more important—quantity or quality?

Is There Any Money in It?

The sad reality is that, unless you work as a permanent staff reviewer for a major newspaper or publication, there's little chance of making any money reviewing. Sure, there are some publications that pay anywhere from $50-$250 per review (see the Resources section in Part 3), but they are usually serious review publications dealing with serious literary books and not genre fiction. Most online review sites don't pay. Most reviewers are unpaid volunteers. Your payment as a reviewer is the book and the chance to see your review published for the public to read.

Reviewers may also get paid in author copies, or are given a choice between a small monetary payment (like $10) or a one-year subscription to the publication. The good news is that, if you're good, you may get invited by the editor to write more reviews and even longer pieces like articles. This is a great form of payment if you also happen to be an author, bringing you exposure and publicity. Writing for prestigious review publications, even if they don't pay, is a fabulous way to build your reputation and credibility as a professional reviewer, and to add credits to your resume. If you're quoted on the front or back cover of a book with your name on it, this is great free publicity for your own work.

But money? Take it from Jim Cox, editor at *Midwest Book Review*: "Here is the secret to being financially successful as a book reviewer—marry rich."

What's in It for You, the Reviewer?

That sounds like a simple enough question. Right? But it isn't.

When you decide to take up reviewing, you have some thinking to do. Do you want to give up a lot of your free time? Because you will do just that. Or, do you want to commit yourself to reading books you'd normally never pick up? Because you will.

Those are only two of the things to consider. How about making yourself sit down to write a review on a day when you'd rather be outside or watching television or visiting friends, etc. Because you will have to do that, too. There will be times when you've just read the most boring book in the world or the slowest or the most poorly written, but you will have committed yourself to giving a review of the book to whoever sent it to you.

You owe the review in exchange for having been given the book to read. It's the same as a bill for merchandise. You make the deal and must carry through your part of it if you want to be thought of as honest.

If you like to read for fun or self-education, once you take up reviewing, you will need to find another hobby because there will be times when you will absolutely not want to look at another book. That will not necessarily be the result of any poor book or any great book you've read, it will merely be your brain needing or demanding a break, your mind needing a change of pace. So you will definitely have to decide how many books you want to read in a given time.

Some of this depends on how many books you can read in a month, for instance. You will need a certain amount of time to write one review for one book. The better the book, the easier the review is to write, but not all books will be in that category. Many of them will be in some middle ground you set and some on the lower level of not very good. The poorer the book, the longer it may take to write the review since you will want to try to be as positive as possible while at the same time saying how poor the book is and why you think so.

You must think through very carefully the decision to become a reviewer because of the possibilities it presents.

If you are willing to work, and reviewing is work, and you have the self-discipline to do the job, reviewing has its rewards.

The first such reward, obviously, is you receive reading material. The book, ebook, or ARC is sent to you as 'payment' for your time and effort in writing the review. Depending on the number of books you review, you can build up quite a nice library in a few years.

Another reward from reviewing is, if you are an author, it helps develop name recognition. However, do not make a practice of reviewing books for the publisher of your own book. Such reviews are often called sales hype, especially if they tend to praise the author. Name recognition comes from having people read your reviews and gradually come to remember they liked a book they got as a result of one of your reviews. This will have them looking at other reviews you write and taking your word that a book is good or not. Name recognition from reviewing can result in sales of your book to these same readers.

If you are an honest reviewer who writes positive but honest reviews, you may develop a following and you will also have certain people or publishers requesting you to read their books. This again is name recognition and becoming known. You may eventually find an opportunity to have your reviews printed in magazines. Many reviewers who start reviewing books for small online sites can end up being published by prestigious and well-respected print publications.

A final reward and, perhaps the most important, is having the opportunity to share your views with others about a book, helping a good author sell a good book, thus helping them build a reputation. That's a great source of satisfaction.

This brings you back to the original question of why you'd want to be a reviewer. If you are looking for power in some form, as a reviewer you will have power if you use it wisely. If you use it in a negative manner by writing negative reviews because some misguided person told you that was the purpose of reviews, the power won't last long and you won't be respected by authors. If you use the power in a positive manner, it will grow and you can have a lasting influence and be well respected, particularly if you are honest in all your writings.

Once you've decided to try reviewing, relax and enjoy the experience. There's nothing else quite like it.

Dealing with Review Editors, Authors, Publishers and Publicists

Not every book you receive to review will be an enjoyable read. It will not meet certain standards you've set in the rating of a book or it may just be a book you would not choose as a personal pleasure read. However, in your dealings with people who send you books—be they an author, publisher, publicist, or review editor—you must be fair and objective. And still, you will not be able to please them all.

When a misunderstanding arises, handle it with as much tact and diplomacy as you can. You will soon develop a reputation as a reviewer with whom, while not always rating books high, it is easy to communicate.

Some of the most common problems are:

Problem:
Angry author/publisher/publicist sends you an email expressing their displeasure at a negative review.

How to Handle:
If it's just an irate email because the person feels you were unfair with your review, answer tactfully and state that, although you can sympathize with them, you still feel the book didn't work for you. (You may restate your reasons.) Do not change your review just because someone asks—or begs—you to do so. This defeats the purpose of the review and will reflect on your integrity as a reviewer.

Sometimes the person will resort to the telephone instead of email or letter. Let them know they are being listened to, but don't give in and don't change your rating of the book, no matter their insistence. If they start berating you or using language you don't like, you have the option of hanging up on them. Do not respond by losing your own temper.

Horror stories are not uncommon—with angry authors and even publicists threatening the reviewer and harassing with countless emails and telephone calls at odd hours of the day, demanding they take down the review. They may demand a new review or that the reviewer be fired.

If the email is offensive, don't answer it a second time if you've responded politely to the first one. Do not allow a running argument to ensue; it is one you will not win. Too often this person wants the last word and this does show a serious lack of judgment on their part. It is best to avoid contact with this person. The same rules apply if this person telephones you.

Here's how Andrea Sisco of *Armchair Interviews* handles angry reactions to negative reviews:

> 1. I listen to their complaint. I try to let them know I hear them. Sometimes, venting is really what they want to do and to know someone hears them fits the bill.

> 2. If it's an email exchange, I respond, but don't become engaged in a volley of increasingly angry emails. (I've learned my lesson and have saved all the emails.) Emails are difficult because you can't hear intonation, etc.

> 3. If it's a telephone call, I listen and let them know I hear their concern and frustration, but firmly tell them we won't get a new reviewer, change ratings, like their book more, lie, or whatever their complaint is. And I always, in some form, talk about a review being one person's opinion.

> 4. I go with the flow. If they're upset and want to vent, it doesn't hurt and might help to listen. But we've had some threatening emails and I've had to tell the person that if they didn't stop it, we would notify the authorities. I copy all the emails. And I notify the reviewer and inform them and instruct them to copy

to me any correspondence (the book is sent to them, so only their address is shown) and not to reply. I will respond. Needless to say, they don't get another review. I have my handy-dandy list (which is really short) and I remember every person who has been nasty to me or our reviewers. Also, we reviewers talk to each other. If I have a bad experience with an author, I'm probably going to share it with another reviewer. As I said, the list is short. When I've become firm, they let it drop. I've even received (later) apologies. I pass those on to the reviewer, if it's not my book. And to disagree with our reviews is fine, but be professional about it. Remember: A review is just one person's opinion.

This is a sample of a negative review reply to an angry author/publicist:

Dear Mr./Mrs./Ms_____:

I am sorry that you are dissatisfied with the review I wrote on the book "_____". I do not mean to insult the author's creative ability nor writing talent, however, there were problems I found in the book that could not be ignored and keep me from recommending it to the readership of the "_____" genre at large.

Examples of reason for negative review:

1. It is apparent that the book was not edited before being published as I found several typographical errors and misspellings and the punctuation seemed to be lacking.

2. There are several pages missing or out of order in the copy I received and I could not follow the story because of it.

3. I found the characters to have no depth. The author told the reader what they were thinking/feeling/seeing and did not allow the characters to tell the reader themselves. I could not develop a bond with the characters, meaning that I simply did not care if they existed or what problems they had. I could not picture them in my mind—did they have black/blond/red hair, green eyes, etc. Were they tall/short, etc. I do not know if they had a family or a sense of humor and so forth.

4. The author was obviously not able to carry out the ambitious plot he set for his story and left too many unanswered questions such as, what happened to the secondary character who..., how did the detective/PI/lawyer reach their conclusions and prove the case? The author introduced a last-minute character to be the villain, a character of whom we had no knowledge as there is no previous mention of him. The author used "Suddenly there was a-" storm, new character, etc., to resolve his problem of how to end the story.

5. The book was written with improper use of the language in places—using peek or peak for pique as an example. Any author should know the meaning of and the spelling of any word they use.

I do wish the author success with his/her next book and please understand, I am only responding to the book as I see it and there is nothing personal in the review.

The author does have talent, I think, and with some study or attention to detail on his/her part, they could write books I'd be happy to review in the future.

Sincerely,

Reviewer's Name

Problem:

An author/publisher/publicist/review editor sends you the book, but you never receive it.

How to handle:

Although this doesn't happen very often, the post office is not perfect and books can get lost in the mail (maybe even more so with reviewers living abroad). Notify the person you haven't received the book after it becomes obvious that something has gone wrong. In the States this would be 2-3 weeks after the person has sent the book. Abroad, this would be up to 5-6 weeks, depending on how the person sent it. More often the books arrive late rather than being lost. Lost books, however, are not the reviewer's responsibility.

Problem:

A review editor 'assigns' you to purchase a book and write a review of it with the 'promise' of publication, but when you submit your review, the editor never answers back and is 'out of the picture'.

How to handle it:

Better to avoid this kind of situation altogether. You shouldn't purchase a book without any real assurance that your review will be published as promised. If you have fallen for this and have spent your money on the book and your time on reading and writing a review, you've been had. Don't be naive. Your main payment as a reviewer is a copy of the book; you should never have to buy your own review copy. If you do, you're paying to be a reviewer instead of the other way around. Let this be an experience that won't happen again.

It is sad, but even review editors of well-known prestigious publications have behaved in this unprofessional manner with freelance reviewers, especially with those reviewers living abroad. The advice? If your first email doesn't get an answer, send a second (emails do end up in cyberspace at times). If the second email doesn't get an answer either, avoid this editor and publication in the future and learn from your mistake. If you're really upset (maybe you spent $25.00 on the hardcover version and many hours reading the book and writing the review), you might also try phoning the editor to discuss the problem. (This is not recommended, however.) Always be diplomatic. If this doesn't work, you can always contact the editor-in-chief of the publication to complain about the review editor (unless they are the same person).

Problem:
You receive in the mail a book you never requested.

How to handle:
Unless you've placed an ad or announcement somewhere offering your services as a reviewer without the wish to be queried first, you have no obligation to review the book. If a person sends you a book anyway after you've said no to their query, you have no obligation to review the book. (This is a problem you will encounter most often with vanity press authors.) Make sure the book wasn't sent to you without notification by a review site for which you write reviews.

Problem:
A person sends you a book, then every few days asks if you've read it.

How to handle:
This is why it's important to let the person know in advance how long it might take you to read the book and write the review. It's okay if the person asks once. Just remind him or her of the time frame you gave. If, however, you promised the person the review in three weeks and it's already been two months, you're at fault here and should send an apology and make your best efforts

to complete the review as soon as possible. If you're not able to write your review in the time agreed on, you should always inform the other party. Maybe some will have no problem with a delay, while others will want to make new arrangements.

Problem:

After receiving a book you requested, you're not able to write the review for whatever reason (health, family or personal problems).

How to handle:

Inform the person of your inability to write the review and offer to mail back the book at your expense.

Problem:

The author or publisher queries you about a romance book, you say yes, then the book turns out to be erotica or worse. Some authors and publishers say that their erotica books are simply romance in the hopes that, once the reviewer receives the book, they won't have any choice but to review it.

How to handle:

Always try to avoid this problem by clearly stating the books you DO and DO NOT consider for review. In the problem mentioned, you have no obligation to review or mail back the book. It's useful to let the person querying know that books sent in the wrong genre will not be reviewed or returned.

In cases where someone sends you a book of a genre you do not review and have told them so, you might want to maintain a list of such names and refuse to review any books for them to avoid this problem in the future.

Should a Reviewer Show a Review
Before Publication?

Though this isn't the norm, there are reputable reviewers and review publications that share their reviews with authors before the review is published. Is this fair? Should the reviewer make sure that no misinterpretation of the author's work has occurred? Doesn't this show a lack of self-confidence from the part of the reviewer? Should a review be modified in any way due to the author's disagreement or request for a change? These are all interesting and controversial questions with many reviewers having conflicting opinions.

This is due partly because of fear of making embarrassing mistakes (plot events, setting, character names, etc.) from the part of the reviewer, and can be easily avoided by the reviewer reading the book carefully and taking notes as necessary.

Misinterpreting the author's view or intent, however, is a different story. Just because the reviewer didn't get the full author's intention in the book, doesn't mean it's the reviewer's fault. Maybe the author wasn't successful in presenting his views or ideas clearly through his writing. This is where trusting your own judgment as a reviewer comes in. If you show your review to the author, his comments may influence your final review. Besides, a book is always open to various interpretations, even those other than the author's. Interpreting a book in your own way is part of the job of being a reviewer. In fact, freedom of interpretation is your right as a reviewer.

If you show your review to the author, what happens if it doesn't favor the book? How do you expect the author to react to a negative review? A review should not be modified just because the author didn't agree with it. An exception to this would be, of course, mistakes about plot events, character names, etc., which, as said before, can be prevented by vigilant reading of the book. But for these corrections to be made, a reviewer doesn't have to show the review to the author first. Once published, the author can point out the errors and then they can be corrected.

Reviewing: Practical Tips to Remember

- Keep your writing style concise, direct and reader-friendly. Don't try to impress readers with fancy words.

- Whenever possible, try to specify the intended readership. Some books are specialized and appeal to only one group of people. Even if the book has some poor qualities, it might still be of interest to some readers. For example, a mediocre novel about the life of a violin player may be of interest to violinists and musicians, something worth mentioning at the end of a non-enthusiastic review.

- Stay away from clichés like "A real page-turner!" "Un-put-down-able!" It's a pity, but even big newspaper reviewers sometimes use these expressions. You see them on the back of paperbacks all the time.

- Don't let a few typos affect your review if the book is good. Even books published by major houses sometimes have small errors. Two or three typos or punctuation mistakes are forgivable—again, if the book is good. But if the spelling mistakes are more than two or three and distract you from the work, you should point that out in your review.

- Be aware that some review publications, print or online, have different preferences when it comes to point of view. Print publications generally dislike the use of the first and second person. They prefer the use of "This reviewer" and "The reader," as it gives the impression of being more objective and detached. Review sites usually are more flexible and some won't care about point of view as long as the review is thoughtful and well-written. Some review sites prefer reviewers to use first person in the evaluative part of the review, thus giving the review a closer, more personal touch.

- Be advised that the most commonly preferred tense when writing a review is the present. Generally, the lead and plot description are written in the present simple and present perfect simple tenses (except when events that took place before the story starts are mentioned, in which case it's okay to use the simple past tense), while the evaluation may combine several tenses, such as simple past, present simple, present perfect simple and/or future simple. Though this seems to be the most accepted format for print reviews, online review sites are more flexible. There are no hard and fast rules here. In the end, a good reviewer knows how to combine the different tenses and still write a clear, well-structured review. Study reviews from well-reputed publications to get a feel of the different tenses used in a review.

- Read different types of reviews to get a feel of what a review should be like. Read in different genres and various types of publications, both print and online. Read the review quotes printed on the back covers. Soon you'll be able to differentiate the well-written reviews from the mediocre.

- Try not to review books from family members, friends or people you know. The less you know about the author or publisher, the less chance of conflict of interest and the more freedom you have to be honest. You're human, after all, and it's not very clever to give a negative review to your author cousin if he comes every year to Christmas dinner. The same with friends. Your friend's book may turn out to be great, but it also may turn out to be a stinker. Why take the chance? An honest review is not enough reason to spoil a friendship. It is best to avoid this kind of situation altogether. Likewise, don't review books from people you hate!

- If you read all kinds of books, then review all kinds of books, but if you mostly read books in one genre, then it's more sensible to only review books in that genre. If you hate fantasy, for instance, then there's no point in reviewing fantasy books. Your reviews will have more insight, more 'meat' when you're familiar with other authors and books in that particular genre. Your awareness of trends and the current market will allow you to compare the book to others in the same field. Likewise, if you have read many books by one particular author, reviewing a new book by this author will let you place his new work within his other body of work, which is always a good touch in a review.

- Try to review books in the order in which you receive them. This will help in keeping up with deadlines and is only fair to the person who submitted it.

- If you plan to review books in all categories, make sure you understand the various types of genres and subgenres. For example, it's embarrassing to complain in your review that a story has highly improbable situations if the story in question happens to be a parody!

- Reading the book and providing the review to be posted or posting the review on at least one site is your basic responsibility as a reviewer. Generally, you'll be requested by the author or publisher to post the review on one or two other sites where the book is sold (ex. Amazon and B&N). If you're familiar with these sites, these additional postings don't take much time, but unless you stated beforehand that you were going to post your reviews on various sites, you're under no obligation to do so unless you want to. Posting reviews on multiple sites can be very time consuming. It is therefore a good idea to build a list of such sites in advance if you plan to post the review on more than one or two sites.

- Don't be prejudiced. Don't assume that a self-published or small press book will be poorly written. Give it a fair chance and let it speak for itself. Likewise, never assume a book published by a major NY house has to be good. You'd be surprised by the high quality of some small press books by unknown authors as opposed to those written by big name authors whose titles are often in the bestseller lists. The fact is, a famous name is the major factor in selling a book, regardless of the book's level of excellence. As a rule, most subsidy books are mediocre and poorly written (of course, there are always exceptions). If you've had bad experiences with subsidy books, then don't request them nor accept them for review. If you decide to review one, though, don't be prejudiced and give it a fair chance.

- Remember that the books are being sent to you in exchange for a review. Accepting books and not writing the reviews is, in one word: STEALING. You'd be surprised at the number of 'reviewers' who, after having requested several books, suddenly 'disappear.' These people are not legitimate, they're crooks, plain and simple. Integrity is part of the code of honor of a legitimate reviewer.

How to Start Your Own Book Review Site

Setting up your own book review site can be an exciting and challenging endeavor, but it is also hard work and requires not only a lot of time and effort but money as well. A successful review site doesn't happen overnight. There are many things you need to consider, plan, and do in order to make the site a success. But if you're good at it, you can end up with a high-traffic site that is well-known among readers and respected by authors, publishers and publicists.

Here are some suggestions to help you get started.

Decide what type of review site you want.

There are many types of review sites. Some specialize in only one genre, some in all types of books. Some have a limited number of reviewers and a small database. Some are huge, with up to one hundred reviewers and enough web space (bandwidth) available for thousands of reviews. Some sell ads to authors and publishers and offer promotion packages and interviews for a fee (the money usually goes to maintaining the site), while others don't. Some charge for reviews (NOT recommended if you want to build a credible reputation!) Usually review sites begin small then, as their names become known to authors, publicists, and publishers, and more reviewers are added, they gain in popularity.

Do you want a site specializing in children's books? Do you want only a few staff reviewers? What type of reviews do you want to publish? Pre-publication, post-publication, or both. Is your aim to make money, too? Is your plan to become an affiliate of an online bookstore and earn commissions? Do you want to sell advertising to cover web hosting/maintenance costs? (This is usually done when the site has acquired some popularity and receives many thousands of hits a month. Also, if you collect money from your site, be ready to learn the business laws which necessitate tax accounts, licensing, bookkeeping, etc., and will differ by country and state.)

Do you want to offer readers something besides reviews, such as author interviews (written or audio), articles, contests, a newsletter, etc.? Do you want books sent directly to you to mail to reviewers, or would you rather have the books sent directly from author/publisher/publicist to the reviewer? (The first scenario is more common with print review publications. Online review sites usually prefer the second option.)

Make sure you consider these questions before you move to the next step. Be certain you want your site to review only mystery books, for instance, before you choose your domain name as this will reflect the focus of your site.

Choosing a domain name

Once you select a domain name for your site, the first thing you need to do is make sure that it is not already taken. If you incorporate or LLC, it is highly recommended that you hire a lawyer to make sure the business name isn't already in use. If the name even comes close to another one, you won't be able to register it.

If you're doing this on your own, check if the name already exists. Places you can check this:

http://www.networksolutions.com/whois/index.jsp
http://www.domaincentral.com.au
http://www.godaddy.com
http://www.OOOdomains.com

The price to secure your own domain name is about $10. Try to choose a name that matches the tone and focus of your site and that is original and easy to remember. Most often a host will get your domain name for you when you choose them as host. They usually include the cost of the domain name in your price. The domain is registered in your name, however, and not theirs. (As a word of warning, you shouldn't renew your domain name with an agency other than your host. In many cases you may wind up changing to another registry than the one your host uses and end up paying twice for the same domain name. Also, you should realize that some hosts will register the domain name for you, but it will be in their name, not yours. So check this out before deciding on a server.)

Keep your budget in mind

Starting a review site that looks professional and runs effectively costs money, sometimes LOTS of money. As mentioned before, if you incorporate or LLC, there's the cost of legal work and an attorney, which can run about $1,000. Getting a web designer, host, logo and banners, enough bandwidth to handle many reviews and all the other aspects of running a website (including computer programs to load reviews) can cost from $5,000 to $10,000. It can be done for less, but keep in mind that most of the time what you spend on your site will reflect on it too. If you hire an amateur to do the work, your site may suffer for it. Even worse, if you try to design the site on your own, it might end up looking amateurish and be difficult to navigate. In the end, what matters is the final product. So whether you hire a professional, use the services of an amateur, or do it yourself, make sure your site is user-friendly and looks professional. Review copies are expensive (unless they are ebooks, which cost nothing) and authors, publishers and publicists won't send copies to a review site that doesn't look professional. If you are computer savvy, you might be able to design and maintain your site and possibly save thousands of dollars. But if you do it yourself instead of hiring someone else, be ready to spend a lot of time at the computer. You may have to spend anywhere from twenty to fifty hours a week on maintenance alone. If the job becomes too time consuming, you may need to hire someone to post reviews and assign books.

If you're able to design and maintain a site on your own, you'll still need a web hosting company (more on this below).

Keep in mind that, as a rule, review site owners don't get rich. The money earned on affiliate sales (with Amazon, it is about 4%-8.5% per title purchased, depending on the amount of books sold) and ads will usually go to the maintaining of the site and often are more trouble than they're worth. In the end, the amount of money you earn will depend on the type of product or service you sell. Some review sites offer editing services and high-priced promotional packages, and, as mentioned earlier, some charge for reviews or for having them done in a certain time frame—the so-called 'express' reviews.

As a last note, be aware that authors and publishers are often wary of review sites that sell their services and especially distrustful of review sites that charge for their reviews, even if they are 'express.' If you decide to charge for reviews get ready to receive negative criticism and to expect a very low response from authors, publishers and publicists. Why should a person pay for a review when there are so many respected review sites out there that won't charge a penny? Even with well-known, prestigious review publications like *Kirkus* who charge the staggering amount of $425 for their *Kirkus Discoveries* section, people's perception on this is far from positive.

One thing is for sure: no paid review holds the same credibility as a free one. Once a person pays you money for a review it's difficult to remain objective. Money becomes an issue. Chances are you'll be discouraged from writing a negative review if you want the same author or publisher to come to you for another review in the future. The bottom line is, if you want to become known as a serious reviewer, charging for reviews is a bad idea. Maybe this perception will change in the future, but this is how it is now.

There are some sites that charge a fee, not for the reviews themselves, but in order to pay for staff members to post and handle reviews. This is in no way the same as charging for a review.

Selecting an Internet Service Provider (ISP)

You will need this in order to connect to the Internet and have an email account. The best well known ISPs are CompuServe, AOL, Earthlink, MSN and AT&T, but there are many others.

Designing your website

What look would you like your website to have? Dark and mysterious? Fun and colorful? Streamlined and businesslike? Check other sites you like and incorporate those qualities in your own. Whatever the style, make sure the site will be easy to navigate and keep download time to a minimum. If you decide to hire someone to design your website, check other websites the designer has done. On average, prices can range anywhere from a couple of hundred to over a thousand dollars.

If you decide to design it yourself, keep in mind that, in most cases, a website designed by an amateur will show it. However, if you want to save money, there are some programs to guide you such as Microsoft FrontPage, Net Objects Fusion or Macromedia Dreamweaver (not recommended for beginners). http://www. WebDesign.about.com is a helpful site to check.

Selecting a web-hosting company

This is very important. Be sure to spend time examining the different options and choosing a hosting company that is trust-worthy, high-powered and has dependable customer service. For a list of web hosting companies, check http://www.hostin-dex.com that lists the top twenty-five in order of popularity.

Normally, your hosting company will list your website with all the major search engines.

Become an affiliate

When you become an affiliate, you earn a commission when people who browse your website click on your links to online retailers and buy the books. The Amazon program seems to be popular among review sites, easy to deal with and not as time consuming as other retailers.

The commission can be from 4% to 10%, depending on the number of books sold.

For more information on the Amazon Affiliates program: http://affiliate-program.amazon.com/gp/associates/join

For the Barnes and Noble Affiliate program: http://www.barnesandnoble.com/affiliate/intro.asp?z=y

For the BooksaMillion Affiliate program: http://www.booksamillion.com/ncom/books/affiliates/marketing_tips?id=3557033236560

Among other retailers who offer affiliate programs are Abebooks.com, Alibris.com, Bookcloseouts.com, Half.com, Powell's Books.com. Contact their sites for more information.

Though the money earned from these programs is rarely more than 'pin' money, it can come in handy for paying hosting and maintenance fees.

Define your rules/guidelines

This is one of the most important things you can do for your site.

Ask yourself these questions: Will you keep archives of old reviews? How long will a review remain on the site? Who will own the rights to the reviews—you or the reviewer? Will you allow reviewers to post their reviews elsewhere? (Reviews are the intellectual property of the reviewer and without clarification of their use a lot of trouble can ensue.) Will you consider freelance reviewers or will you only publish reviews from staff reviewers? What genres will you consider? Will you review ebooks as well? How many staff reviewers would you like to have? Under what circumstances would you need to fire a reviewer? What style of review would you want your reviewers to write—short and light or long and in-depth? (You'll need to set guidelines for your reviews.) What will be the minimum and maximum word count? Will you edit the reviewers' reviews for spelling, grammar, or word-count before posting? Will you read them for acceptability of posting? What will be your turn-around for reviews? Two weeks? Three? One month? Will you request review copies to be sent directly to you, to be later sent to reviewers? Or will you have the books sent directly from the author or publisher to the reviewer? What will be your criteria when recruiting reviewers? How many books will you allow the reviewers to request at one time?

Make sure you have all the bases covered. Spend some time studying what other review sites are doing and copy what you like and think would work for you.

Recruiting reviewers

According to Maggie Ball (http://www.compulsivereader. com), it's probably best to review on your own for some months before actually starting to recruit other reviewers. Once you decide you're ready to start hiring or taking volunteers, don't get carried away and accept anybody who volunteers for the job. Try to be selective. Dealing with reviewers is one of the most difficult aspects of managing a review site.

"In my experience, coordinating with reviewers is most difficult," says Tami Brady (http://www.tcm-ca.com). "It's hard to recruit good reviewers. It's hard to tell who will be a good reviewer. Some of those who sound great on paper and had excellent clips soaked us for a load of books and never handed in reviews. Others who had no experience but just loved reading have ended up being some of our most well written, consistent, dependable reviewers."

If you accept the wrong reviewers, you will end up spending a lot of time chasing them to notify you that a book has arrived and chasing them for late reviews, and they might leave your telephone calls or emails unanswered—if you have ninety reviewers under your charge, it could easily turn to chaos! "They impact your time and your relationships with authors/publishers/publicists," says Andrea Sisco (http://www.armchairinterviews.com). In other words, they become an expensive part of the business.

When a reviewer contacts you asking to be recruited as a staff reviewer, there are some steps you can take to try to make sure that the person is right for the job.

If the person has reviewing experience, ask for some samples of his or her work, as well as some references. If the reviewer has worked for other sites, contact the site owners/review editors and ask them about the person's method of working, dependability and professionalism. Needless to say, if you receive negative comments, it's best not to use this person.

If the person is a beginner without experience, you can always give him/her a chance to see how it goes. Let them review a book or two and observe the way they work. Make sure they read your reviewing guidelines and are aware of your policies. As stated before, a beginner who loves books and writes well may end up being one of your best reviewers.

One last tip: Before putting an ad on your site advertising your wish to recruit reviewers, consider recruiting 'solid' reviewers close to where you live—from your church, book club, bookshop, library, even your neighborhood. Wait until you begin to expand to post that ad. This might save you a lot of trouble in the beginning—it's easier dealing with 'flesh and blood' reviewers you can physically meet with instead of 'virtual' reviewers who may take off with the review copies and vanish into cyberspace!

Making contact with authors/publishers/publicists

If you're an aspiring reviewer, it is HIGHLY recommended that before starting your own review site, you begin by posting your reviews on other review sites or blogs. This way you can start making a name for yourself and become acquainted with authors and publishers before having to spend a fortune on web design, hosting and maintenance. There are many review sites out there where reviewers may start posting their reviews. (A list of these is given in the *Resources* section.) Sites like http://blogger.com, http://wordpress.com, and http://livejournal.com allow reviewers to manage a review blog—and build up a name—without too much effort.

If, on the other hand, you have been reviewing for some time, either as a freelance or as a staff reviewer for some other site, there's a good chance that your name might be familiar to some authors, publishers and publicists. This will make it easier when you open your own review site, as these people will already recognize you as someone who is professional and can be trusted. Chances are you already have a bunch of people who regularly send you review requests and you feel comfortable requesting copies from these people yourself.

This is why it's advisable—in fact, almost a pre-requisite—to become a reviewer before starting your own site. If your name is unknown and you've had no experience, there's little chance that authors, publishers and publicists will send you books—at least in the beginning. As said before, review copies are expensive and people (especially from the big NY houses) will not send just 'anyone' a copy. They need to know the reviewer is dependable. They also need to know they're dealing with a professional-looking site that has decent traffic. As your site's reputation increases, chances are you will receive more review requests.

"Getting review requests is a matter of building up the site's reputation," says Tami Brady (http://www.tcm-ca.com). "I had reviewed for a while before I started up the site so I had a bunch of publicists and publishers who regularly sent me requests anyways so the transition was pretty smooth."

"Personally, I don't recommend someone without a pre-existing track record of reviewing to start their own site," says Maggie Ball (http://www.compulsivereader.com). "You need to *already* have a profile and contact with the publishers. Then each publisher differs in how they want you to request—some ask for a faxed request on letterhead, others allow email requests, and others use a standard request form. You have to check the requirements on the Internet for each specific publisher. Again, no one will send books to an unknown reviewer with a new site that has no reviews on it. You need to work for someone first so you can send clips. Then create the site, put up the reviews, get traffic, and then send out requests."

Another point to keep in mind is that, in the beginning, it'll probably be best to have all books sent to you and for you to parcel out the books to reviewers. Publishers and publicists will not be open to the idea of sending review copies around the world if you're a new site. Later, as your site gains a reputation, you may change this.

Here are some tips for beginners:

Go to all publishers—big, small, electronic (if you will also review ebooks)—and peruse their sites, paying special attention to their review-copy request guidelines. Most will include contact information. Send them a letter/email introducing yourself and your site and make a request.

Do a search on the Internet for writers' sites, forums, groups, and newsletters where authors often post review requests. There are thousands of these online. Then all you need to do is contact the person and ask for a review copy.

Among these are the following groups:

Available Books
http://www.groups.yahoo.com/group/available-ebooks

Book of the Day
http://www.groups.yahoo.com/group/BookoftheDay

Independent Book Reviews
http://www.groups.yahoo.com/group/Independent-Book-Reviews

My Books Out
http://www.groups.yahoo.com/group/MyBooksOut

Poetry and Book Reviews
http://www.groups.yahoo.com/group/Poetry_and_Book_Reviews

Post a Page
http://www.groups.yahoo.com/group/Post-A-Page

Reviewers Choice
http://www.groups.yahoo.com/group/ReviewersChoice

Carols Book Reviews
http://www.groups.yahoo.com/group/CarolsBookReviews

Book Exclusives
http://pubproauthors.bravehost.com/index.html

The Writer Gazette, http://www.writergazette.com, has a section where authors regularly post review requests: http://wgbookreviews.blogspot.com

Keeping a log

Once you start receiving review requests, recruiting reviewers, and matching titles with reviewers, you'll need to keep a thorough record of names, titles and dates. This is where the magical power of a log comes in.

You'll need to keep records of:

- Contact person (including full contact information).

- Title of book and name of author.

- Name of reviewer to whom the book was sent.

- Date the reviewer received the book (Note: a reviewer should always notify you when he/she got the book!)

- Due date for the review.

- Date the reviewer sent you the review.

- Date you posted the review on the site.

- Date you sent a copy of the review to the contact person. (Some publishers request two written copies of the review.) You may want to keep information about postage and cost of envelopes for your records.

Though there's no specific program designed for review sites, Excel and Access spreadsheets seem to be the most used, though not very popular with those who are on the edge of the 'electronically challenged.' With Excel, for instance, you may view what reviews are due for the end of the month. Some sites also use the file system on the Yahoo groups to manage the records. Old-fashioned lists and hard copies may work in the beginning, but once your site starts growing, you'll need something more 'technologically' advanced.

Promoting your site

Congratulations! You have gotten through all the mechanics of creating a book review site. Now you have to spread the word. How do you get readers to visit your site? How do you bring traffic? There are many books on promotion which might prove helpful in building site recognition.

You should list your site in as many review site directories as possible. You may also consider posting (for a fee) banner ads on other high-traffic readers sites, including big publishers' websites. Amazon used to be a place where review sites could post their reviews and build more name recognition but, unfortunately, as said before, Amazon now claims ownership of all reviews posted and you must have a purchasing account with them to post reviews.

One of the most powerful promotional tools you can use is a newsletter. A newsletter is a must for building your site's reputation and spreading its name. You'd be surprised how fast different people can learn about your site via newsletters. Make it monthly, keep it short and interesting and make sure to offer readers something to make reading it worth their time, like contests or free giveaways. Also, exchange listing your site/newsletter with other sites/newsletters so you will be listed on as many as possible. Check frequently for new places to list your review site/newsletter. Another powerful tool for building name recognition is awards. Tell your readers to nominate your site for awards or, if allowed, nominate it yourself. The Writer's Digest's 101 Best Websites for Writers Award is one for which to strive.

Setting up a review site is not for someone who does not want to commit large chunks of time to the task of upkeep and making changes to the site. Updates will be almost daily and you'll have to handle your email quickly to respond to review requests.

You will have to learn to judge when to accept a book and when not. You may be open to self-published books or vanity press books and find to your sorrow they are not well written or edited. At other times you may find this type of book is well written and worth your time.

You will have to identify those printers of self-published books and those of vanity presses who do or do not turn out a well-done book as your review may cause people to spend money on a book that isn't worth their time or money. Any review you post will affect your site and its reputation so you must be selective in reviewers and reviews.

If you consider the information contained in this section carefully, it will help you develop your site without making costly mistakes in time or money.

Remember, it takes time to develop a site and its reputation. There is a lot of competition and sites open and close regularly for many reasons, the main one being the commitment of the time required to keeping it working. The better known your site becomes, the more time it will take.

Once you make the decision to set up your site and are willing to commit the time and effort required, remember to add patience to the mix and you'll be all set.

Good luck.

Reviewers vs. Bloggers: the Controversy

Reviewing seems to have become a hot subject among blog-gers lately, with bloggers being accused by librarians and other 'professional' reviewers of not being objective, honest enough with their reviews, of not posting enough negative reviews and of lacing their positive reviews with facile praise.

The main question seems to be: is it possible to be unbi-ased in a cozy environment where the people who post friendly comments under the bloggers' posts are often the same people who request reviews from these bloggers? In other words, is it possible to be objective in the blogosphere, where authors, pub-lishers, publicists, reviewers and librarians often are on friendly terms with each other in such blog communities as Live Journal? Is this always a bad thing?

In a perfect world a reviewer should never review a book by a person he/she knows. But, as usual, more often than not, what is ideal in theory is not realistic in the real world, and this 'sin' is not only committed by bloggers, but also by legitimate review-ers who write for online and print review publications.

"It's true that some of the books that are sent to me to review were brought to my attention by the authors themselves," says Marcela Landres, editor of *Latinidad* (http://groups/yahoo. com/group/marcelalandres/). "But I consider this as positive—authors who are proactive in the promotion of their book, in-cluding pitching their work to reviewers, are smart and their efforts should be rewarded, not criticized. Otherwise, who am I to rely on for recommendations of books to review—publicists? Their opinions are hardly objective, they get paid to say nice things about every book the publishing company puts out."

Another issue seems to be the lack of format which many (maybe most?) bloggers have when writing reviews. Unlike the 'legitimate' reviewers who seem to have a preference for a stan-dard structure—an interesting lead/opening sentence, a short summary of the plot without ever giving away spoilers or the ending, and an intelligent, fair, tactful evaluation—the bloggers write about books using any format they want. They have the freedom to write in any length or style without a thought about format—even to the point of giving away spoilers or relating the ending of a book. This freedom comes with the territory of being a blogger. In fact, this unpretentious, freewheeling approach is their main charm.

But then, the questions arise...Are bloggers real reviewers? What defines a review? After all, there are many types of reviews—academic and long, light and short, and snippets like those in such publications as *Library Journal.* Different review sites and publications have different guidelines. Are blogger reviews a new, different type of review? Should we draw a distinction between bloggers who are simply readers and post reader reviews and 'legitimate' reviewers who post 'real' reviews on their blogs? After all, just like on Amazon, there are reader reviews and reviewer reviews. Are bloggers the lowly counterparts of legitimate reviewers? Is this an elitist attitude?

These are fascinating questions because there are no easy answers.

A couple of years ago, this dilemma started with the emerging online reviewers who were often accused of unprofessionalism. Online review sites have come a long way since then, in spite of the fact that there are still many amateur online reviewers out there. This has been heightened by the fact that now more than ever, newspapers across the country are cutting down on book review sections and obtaining their reviews from news wire services, forcing authors, publishers and publicists to turn more and more to the Internet for reviews.

Ultimately, not enough credit is being given to the discerning reader of reviews. It's so easy to tell a good review from a cheesy one guilty of facile praise. One must not generalize and put bloggers under one category alone. Just like there are good and bad

reviewers, there are good and bad bloggers. Serious blogger reviewers aren't going to be stupid enough to post overly-positive
reviews because if the reader buys a book based on that review
and then finds that book to be poorly written, that blogger will
lose all credibility and that reader won't come back to this blogger for more reviews. As said before, honesty and fairness are
part of the job of being a reviewer. Yet many bloggers aren't this
serious, a fact that is evident from their sugar-coated, overly-
positive reviews. In the end, it's the bloggers who are harming
themselves and their reputation.

As to the accusation that bloggers don't write enough negative reviews, like with many online reviewers, the general opinion seems to be that there are too many good books out there to
be spending time writing about the bad ones.

"As an author and someone who writes reviews for various
online magazines or websites, I have to say that in the end, it
is always subjective as to whether a review is 'professional' or
not," says Cheryl Kaye Tardif, author of *Whale Song*. "What are
we really doing anyway? We're simply endorsing a product and
telling people we either liked it or not. Of course, most reviewers prefer to only publish reviews of books they enjoyed. I have
in the past written reviews for books I have not enjoyed, and I
found that no one really wants to hear that."

Heather Froeschl, *Book Review Journal* (http://www.
bookreviewjournal.blogspot.com), says, "I've been a professional
reviewer for years. It is always a slippery slide. I write honest
reviews and sometimes that means a negative one. I post my
reviews to several sites, including my blog, but rarely spread a
negative one further than the initial site the author asked it to
be placed on."

One thing blogging technology has done is bring books and
literature closer to the public and, let's face it, the average person
is so busy or has such a short attention span that long, insightful
reviews are not the most practical thing in the world. Blogger

reviews are like quick tasty treats of information for people on the run who enjoy reading about books.

In the end, and in spite of the 'slippery' questions mentioned above, the influence of blogger reviews continues to rise and for many authors and publishers these reviews are becoming just as important as newspaper or magazine reviews.

PART TWO
The Influence of Book Reviews

Reviews and Libraries

For librarians, top review publications such as *Publishers Weekly, Kirkus, Library Journal, Booklist, School Library Journal*, etc., play a vital role in the selection of titles. Reviews are the strongest criterion for selection. Like most booksellers, libraries need to know in advance of publication which titles to order so that they can make these titles available to the public as soon as the press releases are out. A positive review in one of these publications may guarantee thousands of library orders, though the range will depend on several other factors such as the popularity of the author, subject matter, and school reading lists and curricula.

Once books are published, librarians take into consideration other criteria before selecting, like bestseller and award lists, patron requests, local authors who've had local events and/or signings, books reviewed in local papers, word-of-mouth from trusted sources, etc. For small libraries, knowledge of the community's likes and dislikes is also important. Small libraries tend to be more local while big libraries have more sources and bigger budgets for selection. For big libraries, which often send recommendations to their branches, reviews wield a lot of influence—though not in the case of famous authors, for obvious reasons.

Librarians often divide their selections into must-have, marginal, and special interest. If the subject matter is very specific, like horse shoeing, for instance, the librarian will search for book reviews about this type of book.

Besides the top review publications mentioned above, librarians may look at the following sources: *New York Times Book Review, Kliatt, VOYA, Horn Book, Bulletin of the Center for*

Children's Books, pre-publication lists from Baker & Taylor and McNaughton, the Brodart B1B2 Service, and Sunday book reviews in local papers depending on the region. These sources are trusted by librarians for their detailed and honest evaluations. Some acquisition librarians will even look at *The New Yorker* and *The Atlantic*, though this happens on a more personal basis.

If a patron requests or suggests a book by an unknown author and press, many librarians will look on Amazon for reviews, as this seems to be the fastest and easiest review resource. The same rule applies to subject specialists, who also have more time to look on the Internet for reviews.

While some librarians look occasionally at small review publications, most will stick consistently to the big ones. Though some will read reviews from online review sites when they receive mailings or email announcements of new publications, rarely do they look on their own for online reviews. One of the reasons is the stigma against most online reviewers and the perception that they are unreliable and prone to facile praise or—as in the case of some of Amazon negative reviews—revenge.

"I tend to think large, established [review publications] like *Kirkus* and *Publishers Weekly* are more reliable," says Robert Anderson, Literature and Fiction Department, Los Angeles Public Library. "Many of the independent online reviews I've seen tend to be overly positive or overly negative...every book cannot be 'the best book I've ever read' or the 'worst ever written,' but it sometimes seems that way when you read online reviews."

Some librarians have their own preferred review and publisher sites—though not coordinated by the library system. Ultimately, the problem seems to be that librarians are busy people and there are a lot more review sources than they can handle. It's more practical and time efficient to read print publications they can carry with them and read anywhere.

It is interesting to note that, while most librarians rely on the major pre-release review publications, many complain that, more often than not, they have been disappointed with a book that was positively reviewed in one of them. Sarabeth Kalajian, of Fruitville Library, Florida, suggests an explanation. "That seems to happen when there is a lot of hype because of the author's reputation, the subject matter is just really hot, or some factor like a film deal in the works.... When you know that many people will purchase the book based solely on the author's reputation, there is a responsibility to alert potential purchasers of the reasons the book is not astounding." The question is, do all reviewers from these top publications subscribe to this philosophy? Do book review editors influence their staff reviewers?

"...even more common is to be disappointed by a book that has been blurbed by a well-known writer one respects," says Laura Kent, San Francisco Public Library, "Friendship circles influence blurbing a lot and I think sometimes writers are perhaps more generous with their blurbs for other writers' books than warranted." This is also a form of facile praise.

Those librarians who do read online reviews stick to those sites which are legitimate and have a serious reputation, such as *Salon* and *Rain Taxi*, among others. They like online sites because they seem to find a wider selection of books there, and not the title everybody else seems to be reviewing.

Reviews and Bookstores

While it's true booksellers look at different criteria when making a decision about which books to stock, reviews are a tremendously useful and helpful factor, especially when in doubt or when the author is unknown. Booksellers select their titles based on their experience and knowledge of the field, what the 'buzz' is, recommendations and feedback from customers. While reviews are sometimes part of the buzz, they may not always be a direct influence. Booksellers also select books based on the author, publisher and subject matter. They look at hotlists, publisher catalogues and recommendations from sales representatives.

Pre-release review publications like the ones mentioned before play an important role in the selection of books, allowing bookstores to order titles in advance of their official release dates, thus making them available to the public immediately after their release. Other publications which seem to be helpful to booksellers are *Books To Watch Out For, Booksense Selections, New York Times Book Review, Lambda Magazine, Foreword Magazine*, and local newspapers. For science fiction and fantasy books *Analog, Asimov's, Infinite Matrix, Locus*, and the *SF* website seem to be popular.

Like librarians, booksellers usually concentrate on the major print review publications because they don't have a lot of free time to search on the Internet for review sites. Among other things, it's a matter of practicality. They rarely read online reviews because they can carry printed material with them and read it anywhere.

Independent bookstore owners seem to be more open when it comes to online review publications, and some actually prefer it. "In general, I respect them better," says Alan Beatts, of Borderland Books. "They're less susceptible to the "Emperor's New Clothes' phenomena and, more often than not, have a directness and enthusiasm that I appreciate."

Booksellers who use online review sources believe there's more selection on the Internet. The Internet levels the playing field for small press books to be reviewed as the larger publications do not generally review them. Also, online review sites allow them to browse for any particular title at any time as opposed to print magazines which only review a few big titles at a time. Another important point, and this is related to the 'more selection' factor, is that most print review publications review the *same* books at practically the *same* time.

In general, though, the majority of booksellers believe that print publications are more reliable and that most online review sites are places full of 'facile praise' with no quality control. "Online sites are 'unknown commodities'," says Derf Maitland of Readers Cafe Bookstore. This perception, however, seems to be changing as more review sites are becoming just as serious and critical as the print publications. *Salon, Rain Taxi, Infinite Matrix, The Compulsive Reader,* and *SF* are some of these highly respected sites. Though it is easy to check Amazon reviews, booksellers are wary of overly-positive reviews posted here, paying particular attention to the person who posted the review and whether or not this person is affiliated to a serious review publication, in which case the review in question carries more weight. Booksellers are also suspicious of overly-negative reviews obviously written by people with personal agendas.

As a rule, a positive review in one of the major pre-release review publications may guarantee thousands of book orders from booksellers. The amount will depend on other factors such as name of the author, subject matter, etc. If the topic is controversial and has general appeal, chances are the book will be ordered in spite of negative reviews. This is especially true in the case of famous authors who have a large following.

As mentioned before, reviews are particularly important when selecting titles from small presses or unknown authors who often don't get reviews in the major pre-release publications. In this case positive reviews play a major role in the bookseller's decision, along with the physical quality of the book itself and its cover. It's interesting to note that, for many booksellers, the number of pages a book has is often important. "To be honest," says Karin Van Eck, a buyer of sci-fi and fantasy for The American Book Center in Holland, "when a new fantasy author is being pushed, the cover and how many pages (the more the better) influence me more than any review or promotional talk can."

Reviews and Publishers

There are some publishers who do not seek reviews for various reasons—staff limitations and time, a policy of letting authors do all promotion work, or perhaps they do not know to whom the review queries should be sent. Often these are publishers whose staff consists of only themselves and maybe one other person and the number of books they turn out is limited. This last item could also be mainly if they are a new publisher just building a book list. However, most publishers do seek some exposure for the titles they publish and this includes getting reviews. It only makes sense as selling books is the publisher's real purpose and their income, unless they are a vanity or subsidy press whose primary sales derives from authors' copies.

Some publishers find reviews worth the effort as readers use them to help select books for their own reading. A positive quote from a known reviewer aids in this manner. Readers often use reviews as guidelines to differentiate between well-written and poorly-written books. Also, reviews help publishers gauge readers' reactions to the books they publish, perhaps affecting the genre or subjects they publish in the future. Publishers also find that reviews published in the right place can help push sales up or even jump-start them. Some publishers think reviews are a good form of advertising as well in that they get the book noticed by visitors or readers.

"Book reviews are critically important to any book that is targeted at a general audience. No publisher can afford to advertise in all the newspapers and magazines which reach a vast audience, so the only major way to reach the most people with the least money is to obtain reviews, interviews, or other notices in newspapers and magazines," says John Kremer, author of *1001 Ways to Market Your Books.*

Can publishers measure effectiveness of reviews in proportion to sales? Probably not in reality, but it has been proven positive reader comments do spur sales to some degree. Positive reviews are considered a factor in sales, but only one among many such as timeliness, genre, how well known is author or publisher, how available is the book, etc. Publishers have found that a book with no reviews posted doesn't sell well at all while reviews posted in sources with a high readership do boost sales. Yet, it has been found that the sheer number of reviews doesn't guarantee sales either.

Some successful publishers swear by the effectiveness of reviews. "Reviews sell books. They are the least expensive and most effective promotion you can possibly do for your book," says Dan Poynter, author of *The Self-Publishing Manual.*

"Any review is a good review," adds John Kremer, "whether the reviewer liked the book or not. Even a bad review helps to bring attention to the book and to fix the book's title in the minds of readers. Many readers will buy a book despite a bad review—if for no other reason than to prove the reviewer wrong."

The average number of reviews sought by publishers varies by book and publishers. Some publishers like to jump start a book with reviews on the release date while others spread them over time. A third group of publishers likes to combine reviews on release date or even a few prior to release followed by several reviews garnered over time. There is no specific number of reviews sought by publishers as it ranges from less than 10 to as many as 200. Obviously, the more the resources publishers have the more print review copies they're able to send out. In the case of ebook publishers who send out electronic copies, a main factor seems to be whether or not there's a staff person available to request and handle reviews.

The book genre or subject often determines how many reviews are sought, as the publisher has to match reviewer to genre or subject to get the quality of review desired. In the end, not all requests end up in reviews. A total of about 25 copies may be sent to casual and professional reviewers, with a return of maybe five to ten reviews per book.

The type of reviewer, site or publication to which these copies are sent depends on readership appropriate to the book and quality of other reviews given or posted. The reviewer of any book must be able to understand the contents of the book and its purpose or the review will fall short and ill serve the publisher or author so therefore the publisher must know to which reviewer, site or publication to send the book for the best reviews. For example, a publication specializing in mathematics would not be able to give a good or fair review to a romance.

Publishers maintain a list of reviewers, sites and publications that will give fair and quality reviews. These have often reviewed for the publisher before. Yet, most publishers are open to querying new sites, reviewers and publications for reviews of their books as opportunities to further spread the word of the books or reach new markets. In seeking reviews, publishers often have a preference for Internet sites and reviewers or exclusively submitting to print media. It often depends on whether the publisher wants to send ebook versions of the book or print versions which may include galleys or Advance Review Copies.

The larger publishers don't need to send as many review copies since their books are generally reviewed in the major pre-release publications. This is a luxury the small press doesn't usually have. As a result, it is the small presses that seek to get their reviews posted on online sites. Books published by vanity or subsidy presses are not considered by pre-release publications so the only review possibilities open to these authors and publishers are online review sites willing to handle reviews of vanity or subsidy press books.

Avoidance is practiced by many publishers that have had problems with reviewers due to an unprofessional attitude. An honest reviewer will give reasons why a book doesn't work for them and never spoil a book by giving the ending as a casual reviewer might. At times, publishers find reviews written by someone who doesn't know how to write a review that might generate negative reader reaction without being meant to do so. Unfortunately, most publishers feel there is little to be done when they have problems with such reviewers.

Thus, if a reviewer would maintain a relationship with any publisher, they must be able and willing to account for negative reviews. Otherwise, that publisher will drop them and in time, that same reviewer might find themselves with a reputation for giving unfair reviews which means online sites that accept outside reviews may not be willing to post them either. While one does not have to give good reviews just to continue reviewing, one must be fair and objective in their reviews.

This is the golden rule to reviewing and will earn the reviewer the respect of those for whom they review.

Reviews and Authors

Of all the people in the writing and publishing industry, the ones who count on and are the most affected by reviews are the authors. Authors seek reviews for several reasons. One of these reasons is mere ego feeding—to know that they're getting approval or plaudits from the reviewers. This type of author would be most likely to seek out acquaintances, friends, family members and reviewers who always give overly-positive reviews.

Generally, however, the majority of authors will seek reviews for reasons such as promoting their books, finding out if their work is pleasing to the reader or to learn what errors they may be making, and just getting their name out before the public rather than simple promotion for sales—this is building name recognition.

With this in mind, several well-known authors were contacted for their input as to the usefulness of reviews to the author. The majority report they find reviews quite useful in several ways, among them is the fact that readers use reviews to make their decision to read a certain book or not. They do not always consider that the review might be negative if there is something in the review that tells them the book might still be of interest to them.

Some authors add that reviews also spread the word about a new book's release and they often use parts or the whole of the review as a quote on their website as a promotional tool. They feel a positive review validates the author's work, thus letting them know what they are doing right.

Still other authors feel reviews do not affect reader's decisions, but that reviews can start a buzz about a book, particularly if the review is posted to sites with a lot of traffic. Many of these same authors say reviews are their first line of publicity because they cannot afford to pay for publicity so a good review does the job for them. Yet other authors feel that positive reviews posted on well-visited sites are more valuable than paid-for publicity.

The general consensus seems to be there is no real way to measure the impact of reviews on sales of a book. Some authors feel good reviews can and do boost sales. These same authors mostly believe a bad review can't really hurt a good book as most readers know a review is still only one reader's opinion.

Some readers buy only certain lines of books or certain authors and feel no need to read reviews, yet other readers refer to sites like *Midwest Book Review* or Amazon to read the reviews before making a decision to purchase a book. There are also readers who buy a book after it is talked about by a celebrity, however, many of these same books are by those celebrities. Thus, the overall results seem to be there is no way to fully determine the impact of reviews on sales except for the feeling a positive review can only help over time.

Authors who seek reviews vary in the number they request as do the publications and sites for these requests. Some authors do not seek reviews at all as their publishers handle them or the author does not believe reviews have any real impact. Other authors send as few as four to six requests while others run as high as 100. Some authors prefer to send to print publications only, some to online sites only, and others use a combination of both. The preference for receiving reviews at any given time also varies. Some authors like to get the reviews all at once for as effective a buzz or promotion of their books as possible on release dates or even shortly before release dates. Yet other authors like to receive reviews over a period of time to keep their book before the visitors to well-visited websites as long as possible. And a third group of authors combines getting reviews when their books come out with others added over a period of time.

As with the numbers of reviews requested by various authors, the publications and sites contacted to request reviews also varies. Many authors prefer print publications as more reputable and reaching a higher number of readers while others use online, high-traffic sites. The third group of authors likes to combine print publications and online, high-traffic sites.

Authors have differing reasons for their decisions on which method to get reviews. There are authors who feel print media is the only really effective source of reviews and that online reviews have little or no effect on promotion or sales of their books. Often these same authors have publishers who submit review requests for them and do so only to print publications with a known readership.

The authors who use online sites and reviewers believe this is the most effective way to spread the word about their books. Those authors who combine print and online reviews feel this is the most promising way to gain attention for their books. One reason given for using online sites instead of print is that the print review is a one-time event and often out of date as the next issue of that publication comes out whereas the online sites retain reviews on their home pages for several days and then in their review archives for several months, thus assuring availability to any reader visiting the site.

The success of using reviews in getting the word out about their books depends a lot on the type of publications and sites and reviewers queried. Authors often have a list of reviewers and sites that gave their previous books a positive review and will contact them first, adding new reviewers later who they feel may also give a fair and objective review.

There are also those authors who will contact reviewers they know or are sure will give them an extra-positive review no matter the quality of the book. Such reviews may produce re-sults but soon a difference can be seen if reviews from review-ers who are more objective disagree with the overly-positive reviews.

Some authors prefer only well-known reviewers or publi-cations, while others will send a copy (usually ebook) to any reviewer who asks.

Many authors send their review queries only to sites or publications related to the genre of their book. Some query sites that offer reviews of several genres or only seek out new reviewers to get fresh feedback on their work.

Ultimately, the feeling seems to be that reviews are worth seeking and useful in different ways to different authors and have varying results on promotion and sales, but without statistical evidence to prove it out. This continued need or desire for reviews by authors and publishers means there will continue to be a demand for objective reviewers with knowledge of turning out a good review, whether negative or positive, depending on their reaction to each book they read.

The only type of reviewer this need for reviews will not encourage authors or publishers to contact is the reviewer who acts or has acted in some unprofessional manner—among them reviewers who are jealous of an author's success, those who reveal endings or clues to spoil a book for the reader or those who write a plainly-nasty review without ever having read the book.

Most authors have encountered at least one such reviewer's work and the general attitude toward it is these reviews are a fact of life and they do nothing about them. However, there are some authors who feel that even a bad review gives their work publicity and sometimes will actually cause sales to rise.

The unprofessional or unfair reviewer will soon lose all credibility and not be reviewing for long. This means to anyone who would become a reviewer and build a reputation in this field, it behooves them to play fair with the authors and publishers who seek you out. Do this, whether a specific review you write is positive or negative and you will gain their respect and continue to be solicited as a reviewer.

Reviews and Publicists

Authors and publishers have a variety of methods to garner reviews for their books, among them is the use of publicists who are either employed by the publisher, a publicity firm, or act as an independent publicist hired by the author. All make use of reviews to introduce a new author or their work to the book-buying public.

A publicist is a paid professional who has the knowledge and experience to choose which manner is best to gain attention for a new author or book, whether print publications, radio, television and Internet—or any combination thereof. The choice will differ according to type or subject of book, author's background and the amount to be spent on the promotion package selected by author or publisher.

Publicists include reviews in their publicity programs for new books. The number varies as well as the review source, depending on the type of book and promotional package chosen for it. This last factor is based on cost.

The determination of the usefulness of reviews by each publicist is according to how they view them and the results they've had. Some feel advance reviews from the top review publications (*Publishers Weekly, Booklist, Library Journal, Foreword Magazine*, etc.) are the most useful for introducing a new author to book buyers. It builds a familiarity with the author's name and work before the actual book is available and may even create a certain demand for it.

For Penny Sansevieri, author of *From Book to Bestseller* and founder of Author Marketing Experts, reviews are the single most effective marketing tool. "...people like what other people like, and book reviews feed right into this psychology. A book review is a great way to garner the attention of your audience. Book reviews are also minimal in cost, for the price of a book and press kit you can potentially get a review into the hands of people who will then be motivated to go out and buy it."

"Reviews hold a lot of weight," stresses Sansevieri, "and what someone else says about your book is 1000 times more effective than what you can say about it!"

The effect of reviews on book sales varies with each author. Neither the number of reviews obtained nor the positive quality of the review guarantees higher sales. Some publicists aren't sure that reviews affect sales at all as they have no way to gauge this. In this instance, the information isn't made available to them and they have no way to judge what causes someone to buy a certain book. However, they do believe reviews in large publications or niche market publications might help sales because some readers are more willing to accept the judgment of a paid reviewer. Publicists do say reviews help in the sale of self-help books, which is a special category, and self-help books are among the best sellers nationwide. Furthermore, positive review quotes may be used as 'blurbs' for the back cover or other promotional material, and blurbs, says Sansevieri, "are eye candy to the consumer."

Now that virtual book tours have become so incredibly popular, reviews are also requested from bloggers as part of the virtual book tour package. "I believe authors thrive on book reviews," says Dorothy Thompson, author and founder of Pump Up Your Book Promotion (http://www.pumpupyourbookpromotion.com), "and that's why we include them on our virtual book tours. It serves two purposes – the authors get a great stop and they also get an added bonus of getting a review which is sometimes hard for them if their publisher has not seen to it that they get them. My best advice to authors is that they aim for the gold – top Amazon reviewers, for example, are like gold if you can snag one to review your book. Get as many reviews as you can and have the reviewers post them at Amazon because, after all, Amazon is the world's largest online book store and that's where a lot of people are going to buy books. Get a top Amazon reviewer to review your book positively and it's like money in the bank."

Publicists obtain a certain number of reviews for each book depending on the promotion package chosen, the type or quality of book and the author's background. Media trends also play a part in how many reviews are sought, usually found in well-known print publications. The number of reviews may run from as few as three to as many as twenty or more, depending on the results the publicist wishes to achieve.

Publicists seek reviews for differing time periods in relation to the promotion package selected. Some prefer to get the reviews all at once to serve as advance publicity for a new book or author. Some like to get several advance reviews followed up by others for perhaps a period of three months after the book's release date. Still other publicists will continue to seek reviews over a longer period to slowly build up an author's name recognition and keep it in the public eye.

Most publicists select review sources based on the type of book/author/publisher/timing and availability. They must decide which review source would be best for each book and may use known reviewers from a list, but at the same time, keep an eye out for new review sources. Also, reviewers are matched to the subject or genre of the book. A romance, for instance, may be sent to publications like *Romantic Times* and *Affaire du Coeur*, literary books to *The Bloomsbury Review* and *Pleiades*, a book by an African-American author may be sent to magazines like *Mosaic*, while a fantasy or horror book may be sent to *Locus*. Well-visited websites and known publications are also used for reviews. Some publicists belong to review query groups where reviewers can request a copy of the book for review.

All reviewers should take note that any reviewer who gives a poorly-written review or acts in an unprofessional manner will be stricken from the list of reviewers by publicists and word probably passed about their poor judgment. While most pub-licists don't have the problem of dealing with unprofessional reviewers, sometimes an author will because the publicist chose that reviewer. This problem can reflect poorly on the publicist as well and cost them clients should an author choose to spread word of his dissatisfaction.

Thus, it is in the reviewer's best interest to be objective and fair in all reviews or pass on such books they don't feel they can review with an open mind. This type of reviewer will be much sought after by publicists and could develop an audience for their reviews as well, influencing the success of books they review. This is a goal worth working for in dealing with publicists and authors and guarantees a reputation of fairness and objectivity for the reviewer.

Reviews and Book Clubs

There are different types of book clubs a reader may join to receive books suited to their reading choices. Among these club types are those dedicated to one genre such as romance or mystery, those that get deep discounts from large publishers and pass some of that discount on to their readers who subscribe by mail; the clubs set up by a publisher to sell only the books published by their house; clubs that choose books for their readers and send them without the reader ordering from a catalog, and online clubs that may offer books they deem worthwhile from smaller publishers.

Clubs that specialize in genre books only or books from a specific publisher do not generally use reviews to choose their offerings. Large clubs that get deep discounts also choose books from large publishers and well-known authors. They do not use reviews for their selections.

The remaining clubs may use reviews to influence their decisions as to what books to select, but not all. In some, this is the choice of the editor-in-charge of selecting books.

Some editors or representatives refuse outright to consider or read reviews because they consider the quality of the reviews lacking or giving undue praise to a book that is flawed in some manner. These people select books from publishers' catalogues or books sent by the author. They or someone on their staff always read the books before selecting them.

Those clubs that do use reviews may do so on a sporadic basis, depending on the person selecting the books for their readers. They may use specific online websites for these reviews or particular publications. Many representatives use Amazon or bookstores' websites to read reviews and other book club websites. Others use print media reviews such as *The New York Times*.

In general, the clubs using reviews do not turn to the print media, but use online sites. This could be to save the cost of buying publications or the speed of the Internet in producing the same information. The clubs using online review sites do not search out individual reviewer's sites, possibly because the reviewers are unknown, the quality of their reviews is unknown, or that there are simply so many such sites for the time available, that it is easier to chose a few that post reviews from more than one person.

Since not many book clubs at present use reviews, and it is unlikely this will change anytime soon, a reviewer should not attempt to slant their reviews toward this area of book buying, opting instead for the general readership that uses review sites to help them decide whether or not a book is worth reading.

Reviews and Readers

The fact is, most people *do* read reviews. Reviews and readers go together like wine and cheese. Before spending money on a book—especially in the case of expensive hard covers—most people turn to reviews to get an idea of the book's quality and whether or not there's a recommendation. In this age of computers when almost every person has a PC at home, it's easy for booklovers to access the Internet and read book reviews. Furthermore, with the rise of so many niche review sites, and freelance reviewers and readers posting reviews online, it's popular to read reviews.

In their book, *The Complete Guide to Self-Publishing*, experts Tom and Marilyn Ross write, "Book reviews are often regarded as the most persuasive book-buying influence of all."

Reviews play an important part on whether or not a person buys a book; a positive review tells the reader that the money they will spend on that book is worth it, while a negative review will do the opposite and may influence the person into not buying the book. There are times when a person will buy a book in spite of a negative review, but this usually happens when the author is famous and the person is a fan. There are other times when a review may not have an influence, such as when a person is looking for a book on a specific subject and there are not many other books written on that subject to choose from.

A poll conducted shows how influential reviews are to the consumer. Three questions were posed to a group of one hundred people from slightly different backgrounds (mostly educated readers). Below are the questions and their answers.

Do you read reviews to select your reading material?

Always 18%
Sometimes 74%
Never 8%

How much influence does a review have on your purchase of a book?

A lot 34%
Some 56%
None 10%

Will a bad review deter you from buying a book?

Never 22%
Sometimes 62%
Always 16%

While people may turn to different sources to read reviews, the most popular these days seem to be Amazon and print publications like the Sunday newspapers which usually carry a book review supplement. In a bookstore, most people examine the book jackets and back covers for review quotes and endorsements, though these are sometimes looked upon with suspicion. Review quotes from serious review publications seem to have more weight. Readers are becoming more and more discerning and able to tell the difference between 'real' reviews and those with a sugar coating.

PART THREE
Resources

How and Where to Get Started Posting Reviews

You're all set and ready to begin reviewing those books...but where will you post them?

The easiest way is to start with the large online bookstores, such as Amazon, Barnes & Noble, BooksaMillion, etc., that accept readers' reviews. Some of these will allow you to post your reviews freely, whether or not you purchased the book from them, while others, will only let you post reviews of books you've bought at their site. Check your favorite retailers for more information, paying particular attention to their ownership rights policies.

Besides online bookstores, there are many other places on the web where you may post your reviews. Some forums may ask you to become a member and/or require registration (in most cases free) before posting. Here is a list of sites to help you get started:

All Readers, http://www.allreaders.com
Authors Den, http://www.authorsden.com
Book Muse, http://www.bookmuse.com
Building Rainbows, http://www.buildingrainbows.com (only kids may freely post reviews)
Epinions, http://www.epinions.com
Habitual Reader, http://www.habitualreader.com
Kids Bookshelf, http://www.kidsbookshelf.com (only kids may freely post reviews)
Knowbetter.com http://knowbetter.com/Default.aspx?tabid=1
New Pages, http://www.newpages.com/bookreviews/reviewer_guidelines.htm

Reader 2, http://www.reader2.com
Reader to Reader, http://www.readertoreader.com
Review Centre, http://www.reviewcentre.com
Romantic Science Fiction & Fantasy Forum, http://www.
romanticsf.com/cgi-bin/yabb2/YaBB.pl
The Book Review, http://thebookreview.gather.com
The Book Revyoo, http://www.bookrevyoo.com
The Internet Book Database, http://www.ibookdb.net
The Juice, http://www.juicespot.ca

Another way to post reviews and begin making a name for yourself, as mentioned before, is by blogging. Create your own blog on sites like the following and start posting those reviews.
http://www.wordpress.com
http://www.blogger.com
http://www.livejournal.com

Online communities allow you to have a blog where you can post your reviews.
http://www.myspace.com
http://www.gather.com
http://redroom.com
http://morganmandelbooks.ning.com
http://shoutlife.com
http://www.facebook.com
You may also submit your reviews to article directories:
http://www.ezinearticles.com
http://www.associatedcontent.com
http://www.a1articles.com
http://www.alumbo.com
http://www.amazines.com
http://www.articledepot.co.uk
http://www.articlecity.com
http://www.pressarticle.com

You must register first for free with these sites before submitting. When you submit your review to these article directories, your review may appear on dozens of other sites, as people search here for content for their ezines, blogs and newsletters. In other words, you're giving permission to these sites to syndicate your review. These sites don't ask for fresh content, so you may submit to them even if your review has been previously published elsewhere.

There are other high-profile sites where you may post your reviews, but first you must apply to become one of their writers. Usually they will ask to see your past credits and/or writing samples before they accept you or not. These sites also have an editorial board who will review/edit your piece before publication. Among popular sites that fall under this category are:

http://www.blogcritics.org
http://www.americanchronicle.com
http://www.english.ohmynews.com
http://www.bloggernews.net.

Sites like these, as well as article directories, get a lot of hits and may bring a lot of traffic to your own site, something very interesting if you also happen to be an author trying to promote your books. Your byline should always include links to your website(s) and blog(s). If your review is particularly well written and of special interest to readers, it may also be picked up for syndication by other publications. For instance, a review on *Blogcritics* may be selected for syndication to http://www.advance.net, which is affiliated to newspapers across the United States, and to http://www.boston.com as well; a review on *American Chronicle* may also appear on *California Chronicle*, *Los Angeles Chronicle*, and *World Sentinel*; a review on *OhMyNewsInternational* may be syndicated to various newspapers in Korea.

Blogcritics and *BloggerNews* ask for fresh content, meaning that you must first submit your piece to them before posting it anywhere else. Once the review has been posted on their site, you're free to submit it elsewhere. Though *OhMyNewsInternational* strongly prefers fresh content, they will consider previously published material as long as you specify where it appeared first. *American Chronicle* is more flexible in this respect and will consider previously published material.

The sites mentioned above don't offer monetary compensation.

If you're interested in getting paid for your reviews and articles, there are also sites where, once accepted, you get paid based on how many hits your review/article gets or how many times people click on the ads on your page. Besides payment, which grows overtime as you keep adding more content, you also get a lot of exposure, as these sites usually receive about 10-20 million hits every month. Among these sites are

http://www.examiner.com
http://www.suite101.com
http://www.today.com
http://www.helium.com.

These are sites where you can build a reputation as a freelance reviewer and make a little money along the way. Please visit these sites to learn about their requirements, contracts, application processes and payment rates. Some of them, like the *Examiner*, have a long and detailed hiring process which includes a background checkup of the applicant.

The following are additional social communities where reviewers can post reviews and rate books. Membership to these communities is free:

aNobii, http://www.anobii.com
Bookwormr, http://www.bookwormr.com

Goodreads, http://www.goodreads.com
Shelfari, http://www.shelfari.com
LibraryThing, http://www.librarything.com (This one offers an 'Early Reviewers' program, where members may receive free review copies in exchange for reviews. For information, visit: http://www.librarything.com/er/list).

In addition, Amazon offers 'Amazon Vine', a program where a selected number of their reviewers receive books (and other products) for review. Visit this link for information: http://forums.prosperotechnologies.com/n/mb/message.asp?webtag=am-custreview&msg=26876.1&&liaagc=y&redirCnt=1.

Print Review Publications

Pre-Publication

The following are the top print review publications that use both staff and volunteer reviewers. To apply for a job as a staff or volunteer reviewer, you may contact the editors. The editors are extremely selective and seem to prefer librarians, but they're always looking for good reviewers. These publications only consider Advance Review Copies or galleys. These publications are so influential, a positive review in one of the first six listed below may guarantee over 1,000 immediate sales in libraries and/ or bookstores. Their job is to inform libraries and booksellers of upcoming releases, this way libraries and booksellers are able to order in advance and have the books available to the public in time for the 'official' release of the titles.

Please note that names, links and contact information are subject to change. GL stands for Guidelines.

Booklist, American Library Association, 50 E. Huron St., Chicago, IL 60611-2729, Ph: 1-800-545-2433; Fax: 312-337-6787. http://www.ala.org/booklist. Brad Hooper (adult), Gillian Engberg (young adult), Stephanie Zwirin (children's) and Mary Ellen Quinn (reference), Book Review Editors. (This publication also considers final books as soon as they're available.) Reviews all kinds of books.

Horn Book Magazine, 56 Roland Street 200, Boston, MA 02129, Ph: 617-628-0225 ext. 4; Fax 617-628-0882; Email: info@hbook. com; http://www.hbook.com. Roger Sutton, Editor in Chief. Reviews children's and young adult titles. Reviewers' guidelines: http://www.hbook.com/aboutus/employment.asp

Kirkus Reviews, VNU US Literary Group, 770 Broadway, New York, NY 10003-9595; 646-654-4602; Fax: 646-654-4706; Email: kirkusrev@kirkusreviews.com; http://www.kirkusreviews.com. Eric Liebetrau, 646-654-4686 (adult titles) and Molly Brown, 646-654-7277 (children's titles), Editors. Reviews all kinds of books except poetry, mass-market paperbacks and picture books for toddlers.

Library Journal, 360 Park Avenue South, 13th Floor, New York, NY 10010-1710, Ph: 646-746-6819; Fax: 646-746-6734. Email: Anna Katterjohn@reedbusiness.com; http://www.libraryjournal.com. Anna Katterjohn, Book Review Editor Assistant. Reviews all kinds of books except textbooks, children's or very technical. Open to Freelance reviewers. Guidelines at: http://www.libraryjournal.com/info/CA6415293.html.

Publishers Weekly, 360 Park Avenue South, 13th Floor, New York, NY 10010-1710, Ph: 646-746-6759; Fax 646-746-6631; http://www.publishersweekly.com. Reviews all kinds of books except reference.

School Library Journal, 360 Park Avenue South, 13th Floor, New York, NY 10010-1710; 646-746-6759; Fax: 646-746-6689; Email: slj@reedbusiness.com; http://www.slj.com. Trevelyn Jones, Book Review Editor. Reviews all books that are appropriate for school library use. All reviewers are librarians and school library media specialists. No payment. GL at http://www.schoollibrary journal.com/info/CA6439488.html.

Major Post-Publication Reviews

The following print publications review finished books. Some of these publications offer payment, while others don't. This information is often not posted on the site, because it depends on the reviewer's experience and credentials, so please query the editors.

American Book Review, School of Arts & Sciences, University of Houston-Victoria, 3007 North Ben Wilson, Victoria, TX 77901; 361-570-4848; http://www.litline.org/ABR. Jeffrey R. DiLeo, Editor. Reviews literary works, poetry and literary criticism.

Choice, The Association of College and Research Libraries, 575 Main Street, Suite 300, Middletown, CT 06457 ; 860-347-6933; http://www.ala.org/ala/acrl/acrlpubs/choice/home.htm. Address the Editorial Dept. Reviewer GL: http://www.ala.org/ala/arcl/arclpubs/choice/inforeview/reviewers.htm

ForeWord Magazine, 129 1//2 East Front Street, Traverse City, MI 49684; 231-933-3699; alex@forewordmagazine.com; http://www.forewordmagazine.com. Alex Moore, Review Editor. Write 'Possible Reviewer' in the subject line of your message.

London Review of Books, 28 Little Russell St., London WC1A 2HN, UK; phone: 44 (0)20 7209 1101; Email: edit@lrb.co.uk; http://www.lrb.co.uk. Posts reviews and indicates they have contributors.

Midwest Book Review, 278 Orchard Dr., Oregon, WI 53575; 608-835-7937; Email: mwbookrevw@aol.com; http://www.midwestbookreview.com. James A. Cox, Editor. Open to freelance reviewers. No payment.

Quill & Quire, 70 The Esplanade, Suite 210, Toronto, Ontario M5E 1R2 Canada; 416-360-4604, ext. 357; http://www.quillandquire.com; sbeattie@quillandquire.com. Steven Beattie,

Review Editor. Reviews only Canadian published books.

Small Press Review, PO Box 100, Paradise, CA 95967-9999; 530-877-6110; Email: info@dustbocks.com; http://www.dustbooks.com. Len Fulton, Editor. GL: http://www.dustbooks.com/sprguide.htm. Open to freelance reviewers.

The Bloomsbury Review, 1553 Platte St., number 206, Denver, CO 80202-1167; 303-455-3123; Email: BloomsB@aol.com; http://www.bloomsburyreview.com. Tom and Marilyn Auer, Editors. Open to freelance reviewers. Pays $10 or with a subscription to their magazine.

The Christian Science Monitor, One Norway Street, Boston, MA 02115; 617-450-2000; http://www.csmonitor.com; Marjorie Kehe, Review Editor. Guidelines: http://www.csmonitor.com/aboutus/guidelines.html. Pays $150-$350.

Small Print Publications Associated With Colleges and Universities

The following are often associated with colleges or universities and seem to be more open to working with freelance reviewers. Their focus, however, is usually on literary works and poetry, and they have a preference for long, academic, in-depth reviews. While some accept freelance reviews, others prefer to assign books. Always query the editors first.

Atlantic Monthly, The, Editorial Office, The Watergate, 600 New Hampshire Ave., N.W., Washington, D.C. 20037; GL: http://www.theatlantic.com/letters/edlet.htm#submissions. No email submissions. Considers long, critical reviews.

Book Forum, 350 Seventh Avenue, New York, NY 10001; http:// www.bookforum.com. 212-475-4000; queries: generalinfo@ bookforum.com. Considers long, critical reviews.

Boston Review, 35 Medford St., Suite 302, Somerville, MA 02143; http://bostonreview.net. GL: http://bostonreview. net/writerguidelines.html. Contact the editors at: editors@ bostonreview.net. Considers freelance reviews, offers assignments. Payment varies.

Cambridge Book Review, Box 222, Cambridge, Wi 53523; http:// www.smallbytes.net/~bobkat/cbr.html. Guidelines: http:// www.smallbytes.net/~bobkat/submit.html. Queries: bobkat@ smallbytes.net. Looks for long, critical reviews. Considers freelance reviews.

Denver Quarterly, Part of University of Denver, Department of English, 2000 East Asbury, Denver, CO 80208. No email submissions. Use address above. http://www.denverquarterly. com.

Georgia Review, The, The University of Georgia, Athens, GA 30602-9009; Email: garev@uga.edu; 1-800-542-3481; http://www.uga.edu/garev. GL: http://www.uga.edu/garev/brguidelines.html. Stephen Corey, Editor. Does publish reviews and indicates it will read freelance submissions.

Hudson Review, The, 684 Park Avenue, New York, NY 10021; http://www.hudsonreview.com. Paula Deitz, Editor. Guidelines: http://www.hudsonreview.com/guidelines.html. Email form on site page: http://www.hudsonreview.com/contact.html.

New England Review, Affiliated with Middlebury College, Middlebury, VT 05753; 800-450-9571; http://cat.middlebury.edu/~nereview. Stephen Donadio, Editor. Reads outside reviews except during summer months. GL: http://cat.middlebury.edu/~nereview/guidelines.html. Do not accept electronic submissions. Use mailing address above for submissions. Email: NEReview@middlebury.edu.

Library Quarterly, The, The University of Chicago Press, Journals Division, P. O. Box 37005, Chicago, IL 60637; contact form: http://www.journals.uchicago.edu/feedback/show. GL: http://www.journals.uchicago.edu/LQ/instruct2.html. Considers freelance reviews.

Malahat Review, University of Victoria, P.O. Box 1700 Stn CSC, Victoria, B.C., Canada V8W 2Y2. http://www.malahatreview.ca. Contact: malahat@uvic.ca. GL: http://www.malahatreview.ca/submission_guidelines.html. No electronic submissions. Send all submissions by mail to the above address. Considers freelance reviews and assigns books. Pays $35.

Pleiades, A Journal of New Writing, Department of English, University of Central Missouri, Warrensburg, MO 64093. Email: pleiades@ucmo.edu. Reviewer GL at http://www.ucmo.edu/englphil/pleiades/guidelines.html. Kevin Prufer, Editor. Does publish reviews and indicates will read freelance reviews.

Poet Lore, The Writer's Center, 4805 Walsh Street, Bethesda, MD 20815. 301-654-8664. Martin Galvin, Review Editor. No email submissions accepted. Email: postmaster@writer.org. Reads unsolicited reviews sent to address above. http://www. writer.org/pubs/poet-lore.asp.

Poetry, Editor: Christian Wiman. 444 North Michigan Avenue, Suite 1850, Chicago, IL 60611. 312-787-7070. Email: editors@ poetrymagazine.org; http://www.poetrymagazine.org. GL: http://www.poetryfoundation.org/poetrymagazine/sub missions.html. No email queries or submissions. Publishes reviews of poetry books and reads outside submissions.

Prairie Schooner, 201 Andrews Hall, PO Box. 880334, University of Nebraska, Lincoln, NE 68588-0334. Editor in Chief Hilda Raz, University of Nebraska-Lincoln and the University of Nebraska Press. No phone number on site. Does read freelance reviews. No electronic submissions. Email: gengelhardt2@unl.edu.

RALPH—The Review of the Arts, Literature, Philosophy, and the Humanities, Box 16719, San Diego, CA 92176. http://www. ralphmag.org; GL: http://www.ralphmag.org/submissions.html. Email: lolitalark@yahoo.com. Considers freelance reviews—use plaintext emails for submissions—no attachments.

Semiotic Review of Books, The, c/o Gary Genosko, Department of Sociology, Lakehead University, 955 Oliver Road, Thunder Bay, Ontario, Canada P7E 5E1; Ph: 807-343-839; http://www. chass.utoronto.ca/epc/srb. GL: http://www.chass.utoronto. ca/epc/srb/srb/contributors.html. Contact Gary Genosko at genosko@lakeheadu.ca. Considers freelance reviews.

World Audience, 303 Park Avenue South #1440, New York, NY 10010-3657. 347-329-3255. http://www.worldaudience.org. Guidelines: http://www.worldaudience.org/submissions.html. Contact: submissions@worldaudience.org. Considers freelance submissions sent via email.

Other Print Publications that Pay for Reviews

Astronomy, Astronomy Book Reviews, P. O. Box 1612, Waukesha, WI 53187. http://www.astronomy.com. Guidelines: http://www.astronomy.com/asy/default.aspx?c=a&id=2130. No freelance reviews accepted. Freelance reviewer may query to write a review on assignment. Pays $200 for reviews.

Chattahoochee Review, The, 2101 Womack Road, Dunwoody, GA 30338-4497. Email: gpccr@gpc.edu; http://www.gpc.edu/~gpccr. GL: http://www.gpc.edu/~gpccr/submissions.php. Pays $50 for reviews. Welcomes freelance reviewers, assigns books.

Dovetail, 775 Simon Greenwell Lane, Boston, KY 40107; 800-530-1596. http://www.dovetailinstitute.org. Contact Mary Helen Rosenbaum, di-ifr@bardstown.com. GL: http://www.dovetail institute.org/writers.html. Pays $15 and two contributor's copies for a book review.

Good Old Boat, 7340 Niagara Lane, North, Maple Grove, MN 55311-2655; 701-952-9433. http://www.goodoldboat.com. Pays $50 for reviews. GL: http://www.goodoldboat.com/writers_guide.html. Has email contacts for individual editors.

High Country News, PO Box 1090, Paonia, CO 81428. http://www.hcn.org. Contact: Ray Ring, Editor. Email: rayring@hcn.org. GL: http://www.hcn.org/about/submissions. Pays $100-$200.

Long Island Woman, P.O. Box 176, Malverne, NY 11565. http://www.liwomanonline.com. Contact: editor@liwomanonline.com. GL: http://www.liwomanonline.com/writersguidelines.html. Freelance or on assignment. Pays $40.

Mosaic Literary Magazine, 314 West 231 St., #470, Bronx, NY 10463; http://www.mosaicmagazine.org. Contact: Ron Kavanaugh, ron@mosaicmagazine.org. http://www.mosaic magazine.org/info.html. Considers freelance reviews and assigns books. Honorarium and 2 copies. Specializes in black and Latino Literature.

The New Writer, P. O. Box 60, Cranbrook Kent TN17 2ZR UK; Phone: 01580 212626. http://www.thenewwriter.com; GL: http://www.thenewwriter.com/guidelines.htm. Contact: editor@thenewwriter.com. Considers freelance reviews on how-to books on writing.

The Threepenny Review, P. O. Box 9131, Berkeley, CA 94709-0131. Email: wlesser@threepennyreview.com; http://www. threepennyreview.com. GL: http://www.threepenny review. com/submissions.html. Pays $400 for long literary reviews. No email submissions.

The Women's Review of Books, http://www.wellesley.edu/ WomensReview. GL: http://www.wcwonline.org/womens review/becomingareviewer.html. Email: Amy Hoffman, Editor, ahoffman@Wellesley.edu. Assigns books to experienced reviewers. Pays: $0.14/word.

The Writer, http://www.writermag.com. Contact: jreich@ writermag.com. GL: http://www.writermag.com/wrt/default. aspx?c=a&id=927. Pays $50 for book reviews.

Tinhouse, P.O. Box 10500, Portland, OR 97296. Guidelines: http://www.tinhouse.com/index.htm. Contact Tonaya at info@tinhouse.com. Considers freelance reviews. Pays $200 for long literary reviews.

A fact about reviews in print publications is that the print publication may have a policy of not using negative reviews to a book published by a publisher that places advertisements with them. The editor in chief or review editor or the print publication itself may determine all content of the clients' reviews will be positive so in applying to these review publishers, the reviewer should bear this in mind.

Online Review Sites and Publications

General

Unlike the small print presses, these sites usually—not always—prefer lighter, shorter reviews. Some of these publications pay for reviews. Remuneration often depends on the reviewer's experience and credentials. Query the editors first. [Note: GL stands for Guidelines.]

Absolute Write, http://www.absolutewrite.com. Email: Editor@absolutewrite.com. GL: http://www.absolutewrite.com/site/submissions.htm. Considers freelance reviews. Pays $10.

All Books Review, http://www.allbookreviews.com. Managing Editor: Shirley Roe. Email: Allbookreviews@aol.com. GL at http://www.allbookreviews.com/Default.aspx?tabid=110. Recruits reviewers.

Armchair Interviews, http://www.armchairinterviews.com. Contact Andrea Sisco, andrea@armchairinterviews.com. Recruits reviewers.

Author Link, http://www.authorlink.com. Guidelines: http://www.authorlink.com/membership/manuscripts.php. Welcomes freelance reviews. Prior free registration required. Contact form on site.

Basil & Spice, http://www.basilandspice.com. GL: http://www.basilandspice.com/be-a-reviewer. Recruits reviewers.

Bella Online – The Voice of Women, http://www.bellaonline.com. GL: http://www.bellaonline.com/misc/joinus. Recruits writers/reviewers.

Bestsellers World, http://www.bestsellersworld.com. GL: http://www.bestsellersworld.reviewerapplication.htm. Welcomes freelance reviews—fill out application. Prior free registration required.

Black Butterfly Review, http://www.blackbutterflyreview.com. Contact: Eleanor S. Shields, Editor at nooney@comcast.net. Recruits reviewers. Specializes in African American fiction.

Book Ideas, http://www.bookideas.com. GL: http://www.bookideas.com/about. Recruits reviewers.

Book Pleasures, http://www.bookpleasures.com. Contact Norm Goldman: bookpleasures@gmail.com. Recruits reviewers. Look for 'Interested in Becoming a Book Pleasures Reviewer?' on left sidebar.

Book Reporter, http://www.bookreporter.com. Guidelines: http://www.tbrnetwork.com/content/reviewer.asp. Recruits reviewers.

Book Review, http://www.bookreview.com. Guidelines: http://www.bookreview.com/reviewer2.htm. Email: zanne@bookreview.com. Recruits reviewers.

Book Slut, http://www.bookslut.com. GL: http://www.bookslut.com/contact.php. Contact: Jessa Crispin, jessa@bookslut.com. Recruits reviewers.

Bookloons, http://www.bookloons.com. Contact Hilary Williamson, Editor. editor@bookloons.com. Recruits reviewers.

BronzeWord Latino Authors, http://authorslatino.com/word press. Contact Jo Ann Hernandez, Editor: BronzeWord1@yahoo. com. Considers freelance reviews. Specializes on Latino books.

BVS Reviews. http://www.bvsreviews.com. Contact: info@ bvsreviews.com. Recruits reviewers.

California Literary Review, http://www.calitreview.com. Query form on contact page for submissions. Paul Comstock, Editor.

Christian Library Journal, http://www.christianlibraryj.org. Christian books. Recruits reviewers. Contact: infor@christian libraryj.org. For reviewer information, click on 'Reviewers' at the top of the page to fill out reviewer application form.

Complete Review, http://www.complete-review.com/main/ main.html. Email: editors@complete-review.com. Appears to use staff reviewers only.

Critique Magazine, http://www.critiquemagazine.com. GL: http://www.critiquemagazine.com/guidelines.html. Considers freelance reviews. Query form on site.

Cross and Quill Newsletter, http://www.cwfi-online.org/index. html. Guidelines: http://www.cwfi-online.org/crossquill.html. Sandy Brooks, Editor. Email: CQArticles@aol.com. Considers freelance reviews.

Curled Up With A Good Book, http://www.curledup.com. Guidelines: http://www.curledup.com/revue4us.htm. Contact: editorial@curledup.com. Recruits reviewers.

Euro-Reviews, http://euroreviews.eu.funpic.de/index.php. GL: http://euroreviews.eu.funpic.de/newreviewer.php. Recruits reviewers. Query form on site.

Faithful Reader, http://www.faithfulreader.com. Contact using online form: http://www.faithfulreader.com/writetous.asp. One of a group of review sites. GL: http://www.tbrnetwork. com/content/reviewer.asp. Recruits reviewers. Specializes in Christian books.

Get Book Reviews, http://www.getbookreviews.com. Contact: info@getbookreviews.com. GL: http://www.getbookreviews. com/reviews.html. Recruits reviewers. Form on site.

Good Reading Magazine, http://www.goodreadingmagazine. com.au. Considers freelance reviews. Contact Rowena Cseh, editor@goodreadingmagazine.com.au.

Gotta Write Reviews, http://www.gottawritenetwork.com. GL: http://www.gottawritenetwork.com/Reviews.html. Recruits reviewers. Form on site.

Heartland Reviews, 410 Delaware, Leavenworth, KS 66048, 913-682-6518. http://www.heartlandreviews.com. Contact Bob Spear, heartlandreviews@kc.rr.com. Recruits reviewers.

How to Tell a Great Story, http://www.howtotellagreatstory. com. Contact Aneeta Sundararaj, Editor: editor@ howtotellagreatstory.com. Considers freelance reviews.

Huntress Book Reviews, http://www.huntressreviews. com. Query: Detra Fitch and Ruth Wilson, at huntress1@ huntressreviews.com. Considers freelance reviews.

In My Hysterical Opinion, http://www.imho-reviews.com. Forum. Registration required before posting reviews.

In The Library Reviews, http://www.inthelibraryreviews. net. Sharyn McGinty, Review Coordinator. Email: inthelibraryreviews@gmail.com. Uses staff reviewers.

January Magazine, http://www.januarymagazine.com. Contact Linda L. Richards, linda@januarymagazine.com. Considers freelance reviewers, assigns books.

LatinoLA, http://latinola.com. GL: http://latinola.com/contribute.php. Considers freelance reviews. Specializes in Latino culture.

Linear Reflections E-Magazine, http://linearreflections.com/index.php?action=current_issue; Contact the editor: naomi@linearreflections.com. GL: http://linearreflections.com/index.php?action=contact. Looking for reviewers.

Long Story Short, http://www.alongstoryshort.net. GL: http://www.alongstoryshort.net/SubmissionGuidelines.html. Email: writingfriend@gmail.com. Considers freelance reviews.

Mom Writer's Literary Magazine, http://www.momwriterslitmag.com. GL: http://www.momwriterslitmag.com/WritersGuidelines.htm. Email: reviews@momwriterslitmag.com. Considers freelance reviews.

Mostly Fiction, http://bookreview.mostlyfiction.com. Contact: Editor@MostlyFiction.com. GL: http://bookreview.mostlyfiction.com/review-team. Recruits reviewers.

MultiCultural Review, http://www.mcreview.com. Guidelines: http://www.mcreview.com/guidelines/index.html. Recruits reviewers, assigns books.

MyShelf, http://www.myshelf.com. GL: http://www.myshelf.com/aboutus//want_reviewers.htm. Recruits reviewers. Email resume: Editor@myshelf.com.

New and Used Books, 119 Park Avenue, Yakima, WA 98902. 509-453-6762. http://www.NewandUsedBooks.com. Email: info@NewandUsedBooks.com. Staff reviewers. Does not read freelance reviews. Query the editor.

Once Written, http://www.oncewritten.com. GL: http://www.oncewritten.com/About/WriteForUs.php. Considers freelance reviews.

Online Review, http://www.onlinereviewofbooks.com/index.html. GL: http://www.onlinereviewofbooks.com/submissions.html; Email: onreview@comcast.net. Considers experienced freelancers, no beginners.

Overbooked, http://www.overbooked.org. Contact Ann Chambers at overbooked1@verizon.net or ann@overbooked.com. Need to become a member to post reviews.

QBR: The Black Book Review, http://www.qbr.com, Harlem Book Fair, PO Box 170, Hastings on Hudson, NY 10706 . Email: info@qbr.com. Considers freelance reviewers.

Rain Taxi, P. O. Box 3840, Minneapolis, MN 55403. http://www.raintaxi.com. GL: http://www.raintaxi.com/reviewer.shtml. Considers freelance reviews. Contact: info@raintaxi.com.

Rambles, Editor Tom Knapp, 1609 Ridgeview Ave., Lancaster, PA 17603. http://www.rambles.net. Reviewers: http://www.rambles.net/enquiries.html. Contact The Editor editor@rambles.net. Recruits reviewers.

Reader Views, http://www.readerviews.com. Guidelines: http://www.readerviews.com/reviewerguidelines.html. Submit: admin@readerviews.com. Recruits reviewers. Use form on site to query.

Readers Room, http://www.readersroom.com. Readers Room Partners: Katherine Sutcliffe, Natalie R. Collins, Rob (Robert N.) Holden. Email: readersroom2@aol.com. Uses staff reviewers. No indication on site that they read freelance reviews.

Reading Group Guides, http://www.readinggroupguides.com. Recruits reviewers. To contact, use form on site: http://www.readinggroupguides.com/content/writeus.asp.

Rebecca's Reads, http://rebeccasreads.com. GL: http://rebeccas reads.com/ReviewerGuidelines.html. Looking for reviewers.

Review the Book, http://reviewthebook.com/index.php. GL: http://reviewthebook.com/index.php/home/reviewerguide lines.html. Looking for reviewers.

Robin Falls Magazine, http://www.robinfalls.com/ robinfallsmagazine.html. Contact April Robins, Editor: robinfalls@yahoo.com. Considers freelance reviews.

Simegen Reviews, http://www.simegen.com. Guidelines: http://www.simegen.com/agreements/revagr.html. Recruits reviewers. Email: reviews@simegen.com.

Salon, http://www.salon.com, 126 Fifth Ave., 4th Floor, New York, NY 10019, Laura Miller, Books Editor. GL: http://www. salon.com/about/submissions. Considers freelance reviews. Email: jpress@salon.com.

Scribe & Quill, http://www.scribequill.net. GL: http://www. scribequill.net/guidelines.html. Contact Sonali T. Sikchi, Book Review Editor at: bookrevieweditor@scribequill.com. Considers freelance reviews. Recruits reviewers.

Seeker Book Reviews, http://www.theseekerbooks.com. Contact Theresa Welsh at Theresa@theseekerbooks.com. Considers freelance reviews.

Strange Horizons Reviews, http://www.strangehorizons.com. GL: http://www.strangehorizons.com/guidelines/reviews. shtml. Contact: reviews@strangehorizons.com. Considers freelance reviews. Pays $20 for long reviews. No payment for short reviews.

TCM Reviews, http://tcm-ca.com. GL: http://tcm-ca.com/ reviewers.html. Recruits reviewers.

The Chick Lit Review, http://chicklitreview.org/default.aspx. GL: http://chicklitreview.org/writersguidelines.aspx. Contact: igreen@chicklitreview.org. Considers freelance reviews. No longer paying $25 as it used to.

The Compulsive Reader, http://www.compulsivereader. com/html. Guidelines: Click on Submissions. Contact Maggie Ball, maggieball@compulsivereader.com. Considers freelance reviews. Recruits reviewers. Prefers long, in-depth reviews.

The Dark Phantom Review, http://thedarkphantom.wordpress. com. Contact Mayra Calvani, Editor: mayra.calvani@gmail.com. Considers freelance reviews.

The Fiction Flyer, http://www.tri-studio.com/ezine.html. Contact Kathe Gogolewski: kgogolewski@sbcglobal.net. Considers freelance reviews.

The Fiction Forum, http://www.fictionforum.net. Guidelines: http://www.fictionforum.net/main/volunteer/contribute. html. Recruits reviewers. Email: contenteditor@fictionforum. net.

Voice in the Dark Ezine, http://www.mysteryfiction.net/ Voiceinthedark.html. Contact Anne K. Edwards, Editor: marboboo@earthlink.net. Considers freelance reviews.

Word Candy, http://www.wordcandy.net. GL: http://www. wordcandy.net/faqs.php. Considers freelance reviews.

Writers and Readers Network, http://www. writersandreadersnetwork.com/index.html. Guidelines: http:// www.writersandreadersnetwork.com/reviews.html. Contact: clyons55@earthlink.net. Considers freelance reviews.

Writing, Etc. http://www.filbertpublishing.com, Box 326, Kandiyohi, MN 56251. Reviews nonfiction books only related to writing. Email: filbertpublishing@filbertpublishing.com.

Science Fiction, Fantasy and Horror

Dark Realms Magazine, 4377 6oth Street, Cleveland, OH 44144 Print Magazine. http://www.monolithgraphics.com/ darkrealms.html.   Contact: goth@monolithgraphics.com. Recruits reviewers. Pays with contributor's copies.

Feoamante, http://www.feoamante.com. GL: http://www.feoa mante.com/FeoNews/guide_lines.html.   Considers   freelance reviewers. Email submissions: feo@feoamante.com.

Horror   World,   http://www.horrorworld.org/index.htm. Guidelines: http://www.horrorworld.org/reviews.htm. Contact Nanci Kalanta, Editor: nancik@optonline.net. Only horror. Considers freelance reviews.

Locus Online, http://www.locusmag.com. Email: online@ locusmag.com.

Rue Morgue Magazine, http://www.rue-morgue.com. Contact: jovanka@rue-morgue.com.

SFBook, http://sfbook.com/index.php. Accepts freelance reviews. Prior registration is necessary.

SFReader, http://www.sfreader.com. GL: http://www.sfreader. com/review_guide.asp. Accepts freelance reviews and recruits staff reviewers. Submit reviews to: webmaster@sfreader.com.

SFSite, http://www.sfsite.com. Contact: Rodger Turner, editor@sfsite.com. Recruits reviewers and considers freelance reviews.

The Eternal Night Science Fiction and Fantasy, http://www. eternalnight.co.uk. Email: methos@eternalnight.co.uk. Considers freelance reviews.

Romance

Affaire De Coeur, (Magazine). Address: Corporate Office, Affaire de Coeur, 3976 Oak Hill Road, Oakland, CA 94605. Email: sseven1@comcast.net. Indications are staff reviews only. http://affairedecoeur.com. Check form page on their website.

All About Romance, Senior Editor/Reviewer: Ellen Micheletti. Staff reviewers. May apply to become a reviewer. Use onsite form. http://www.likesbooks.com/reviewsubmission.html. http://www.likesbooks.com. Email: ellen.micheletti@wku.edu.

Beautiful Reads, http://beautifulreads.com. Contact form: http://bittenbybooks.com/?page_id=20. Rachel Smith, Editor: beautifulreads@gmail.com. Recruits reviewers.

Bitten by Books, http://bittenbybooks.com. Contact form: http://bittenbybooks.com/?page_id=20. Specializes in paranormal romances but also reviews fantasy and horror. Recruits reviewers. Sister site of BeautifulReads.com.

CataRomance, http://cataromance.com/Home_Page. GL: http://groups.yahoo.com/group/CataReviews-pending. Considers freelance reviews and recruits reviewers.

Coffee Time Romance, Co-owners Karen and KarenneLyn (no last names given on site). Have staff reviewers. Open to applicants for reviewers. No freelance reviews read. http://www.coffeetimeromance.com. Email: karen@coffeetimeromance.com.

Love Romances, Co-owner/Head Editor/reviewer: Shaiha. Email: Shaiha@loveromancesandmore.com. Appears to be staff published reviews only. No indication on site to apply to join staff, but you might contact the editor for information. http://www.loveromancesandmore.com.

Paranormal Romance Reviews, http://paranormalromance.org. GL: http://paranormalromance.org/BookReviews.htm. Email: pnr4staff@yahoo.com.

Romantic Times, 55 Bergen St., Brooklyn, NY 11201. 718-237-1097. Email: rtinfo@romantictimes.com. http://www.romantictimes.com. Nancy Collazo, Editor. Reviews all genres except children's books and poetry.

SFFP Romance, http://sffpromance.iwarp.com. Contact Webmistress Sarah at: ladyeclectic@hotmail.com. Recruits reviewers.

The Best Reviews, Managing editor: Kathy Boswell. Contact managing editor for information on becoming a reviewer. Email: Kathy@thebestreviews.com. http://thebestreviews.com.

The Road to Romance, http://www.roadtoromance.ca. Contact Linda Baldwin, Review Coordinator at: Linda.baldwin@comcast.net. Recruits reviewers.

The Romance Review Today, Owner: T. Figueroa; Editor: J. Bowers. Reviews by staff only. Open to reviewer applications. Email: terrie_figueroa@romrevtoday.com. http://www.romrevtoday.com.

The Romance Reader, http://www.theromancereader.com. Contact Dede Anderson, Editor at editor@theromancereader.com. Recruit reviewers.

The Romance Reader's Connection, Editor: Livia. Staff reviewers only. No indication that one can apply to become staff reviewer. Email: admin@theromancereadersconnection.com. http://www.theromancereadersconnection.com.

The Romance Studio, Tina Pavlik, Owner. For review questions contact Simone Grant on onsite form only. Reviews by staff only. May inquire about becoming staff reviewer. Email: Reviews@theromancestudio.com. http://www.theromancestudio.com.

Vampire Romance Books, Considers freelance reviews. Recruits reviewers. Guidelines: http://www.vampireromancebooks.com/contact-us.

Mystery

Iloveamystery, Editor and publisher: Sally Powers. Email: Sallypowers@roadrunner.com. Reviewers are usually regular contributors who have their own page but may email to query submissions. Information on http://www.iloveamysterynewsletter.com/about_us.htm#Welcome.http://www.iloveamysterynewsletter.com.

MurderExpress.net, http://www.murderexpress.net. Contact vieuxdo@earthlink.net. May consider freelance reviews.

Mystery Ink Online, Editor: David Montgomery. Email: davidmontgomery@yahoo.com. Has contributor reviewers. No indication that outside reviews are read or that outside reviewers are considered. http://www.mysteryinkonline.com.

Mystery News, Partnership: Black Raven Press and Lynn Kaczmarek & Chris Aldrich. Email: contact@blackravenpress.com. Uses contributors and claims exclusive rights to reviews. No indication that outside reviews are read or applications to be included on staff considered. http://www.blackravenpress.com.

Mystery Readers Journal, Founder: Janet A. Rudolph. Berkeley, CA. Email: janet@mysteryreaders.org. Will read outside reviews. GL: http://www.mysteryreaders.org/Guidelines.html. http://www.mysteryreaders.org.

New Mystery Reader, Editor: Stephanie Padilla. Email: editor@newmysteryreader.com. Will read freelance reviews. Also seeking volunteers for regular reviews. Query with sample review. http://www.NewMysteryReader.com.

Over My Dead Body, Email: omdb@worldnet.att.net. http://www.overmydeadbody.com. Publishes a variety of fiction and nonfiction. Does publish reviews, but suggest query first. No indication whether staff reviews or will read outside reviews.

Reviewing the Evidence, Editor Sharon Wheeler. Email: shazwuk@reviewingtheevidence.com. Does not accept outside reviews and there is a waiting list of reviewer applicants. http://www.reviewingtheevidence.com.

The Mystery Reader, editor@themysteryreader.com. http://www.themysteryreader.com. Considers freelance reviews.

Children's

Building Rainbows, http://www.buildingrainbows.com. GL: http://www.buildingrainbows.com/add.php. Freelance reviews by children welcome.

Bulletin of the Center for Children's Books, The Johns Hopkins University Press, 2715 North Charles Street, Baltimore, MD 21218-4363 ; http://bccb.lis.illinois.edu/pubguide.html. Contact Deborah Stevenson, Editor. 1-800-548-1784. Email: jlorder@jhupress.jhu.edu. Recruits reviewers.

Children's Literature, http://www.childrenslit.com. Email: CLCDhelp@ixn.com. Recruits reviewers.

Curled Up Kids, http://www.curledupkids.com. GL on parent site, Curled Up With a Good Book, http://www.curledup.com/revue4us.htm. Recruits reviewers.

JacketFlap, Children's Publishing Blog. Email: tgrand@jacketflap.com. http://www.jacketflap.com. Community of children's book bloggers. Must be a member to post. http://www.jacketflap.com/megablog/index.asp.

Kid Magazine Writers, http://www.kidmagwriters.com. GL: http://www.kidmagwriters.com/others/rite4us.htm. Email: editor@kidmagwriters.com. Considers freelance reviews.

Kids Bookshelf, http://www.kidsbookshelf.com. To contact the editor, go to their site and click on 'Contact Us' at the top menu. Considers reviews by children.

Kids Reads, http://www.kidsreads.com. GL: http://www.tbrnetwork.com/content/reviewer.asp. Contact: Editorial@bookreporter.com. Recruits reviewers.

LYRE Review, http://cc.ysu.edu/lyre/lyre_review_index.htm. Contact Rebecca Barnhouse, Editor: rbarnhouse@ysu.edu. Considers freelance reviews. Recruits reviewers.

My Light Magazine, http://mylightmagazine.com. Contact Jennifer Gladen, Editor: editor@mylightmagazine.com. Considers freelance reviews. Catholic publication.

Stories for Children Magazine, Email: storiesforchildren@vsgrenier.com. Open to reader reviews. Also uses staff reviewers. http://storiesforchildrenmagazine.org/default.aspx. To contact, fill the form on this page: http://storiesforchildrenmagazine.org.contactus.aspx.

Teen Reads, http://www.teenreads.com. GL: http://www.tbrnetwork.com/content/reviewer.asp. Contact: Editorial@bookreporter.com. Recruits reviewers.

Voya (Voice of Youth Advocates), Young Adult Library Magazine, 4601 Forbes Blvd, Ste 200, Lanham, MD 20706. 1-888-486-9297. Email: voya@voya.com. http://www.voya.com. Check: http://www.voya.com/Submissions/index.shtml#reviewer for information. Open to reviewer applicants; contact: ibenson@voya.com.

Write What Inspires You, http://www.donnamcdine.com. Contact Donna McDine, Editor: dmcdine@optonline.net. Considers freelance reviewers.

Writing for Children Center, http://writingforchildrencenter. com. GL: http://writingforchildrencenter.com/submissions. Contact Suzanne Lieurance: suzannelieurance@hotmail.com. Considers freelance reviews. Pays a one month's free membership to their club ($27 value).

YA Books Central, http://www.yabookscentral.com. GL: Form on site to submit reviews. http://www.yabookscentral.com/ cfusion/index.cfm?fuseAction=books.newReview. Welcomes freelance reviews.

A Note About Newspapers:

Big city newspapers rarely consider freelance reviewers, even those with experience. They either receive reviews from news wire services, have their own staff reviewers, or invite famous people (often authors) to review for them. More and more across the country newspapers are cutting down on book review sections. Small local newspapers are more willing to consider freelancers and give local writers a chance. You should contact these first. Before contacting newspapers, even the local papers, it is wise to gain some experience and gather credits by reviewing for serious online sites and/or small print publications. Furthermore, big newspapers rarely display reviewer submission guidelines on their sites. Interested reviewers should always query the book editors first, either by email or phone. For a list of newspapers and their book editors' contact information, go to http://www.bookmarket.com/newspapers.htm.

Appendix

Sample of a Press Release

FOR IMMEDIATE RELEASE

CONTACT:

Anne K. Edwards
Telephone Number:
Fax Number:
AnneKEdwards@Yahoo.com
http://www.Mysteryfiction.net

A MOST UNCONVENTIONAL PRIVATE INVESTIGATOR

DEATH ON DELIVERY

November 5, 2004—Hannah Clare, Private Investigator, makes her debut in *Death on Delivery* by Anne K. Edwards.

Hannah was created to offer the reader something different in a private investigator. She is a loving mother and grandmother who enjoys catching killers. She says it gives her a rush.

Hannah resides in a small fictional community of Penn's Crossing located outside of Philadelphia. Her hobby of reading obits brings to her attention a series of deaths due to unknown causes and when the opportunity to investigate arises, she takes it and nearly winds up a murder victim herself.

The creation of Hannah Clare is strongly influenced by Agatha Christie, an author much admired by Anne K. Edwards. Anne likes to know why people commit crimes and writes with that perspective in mind.

The character of Hannah Clare is based on a no-nonsense approach to life, although she admits to being somewhat judgmental about people's characters which give her a human quality along with her lifetime habit of smoking too much. She uses her wits to get out of tight spots as she works alone.

Contrary to many PI novels that portray the police as rigid, sneering types or nearly as bad as the criminals themselves, Hannah finds them to be good people. She is particularly fond of one young policeman and teases him mercilessly about his love life.

What reviewers are saying:

"...a well-written, clever little mystery."—Russel D. McLean, *Crime Scene Scotland*

"...an original, heart-racing mystery!"—*Reader to Reader*

"If you thought that Agatha Christie's Miss Marple was unconventional—Hannah Clare is— well, most unconventional... superb investigation culminating in an exciting finish. More a whydunit than a whodunit—*Death on Delivery* provides an absolute fun read." *New Mystery Reader*

Anne K. Edwards writes in a variety of genres—mystery, speculative, children's, non-fiction. She reviews books for several review sites and is editor of the monthly ezine, *The Voice in the Dark*. For interviews and/or review copies, please contact the author or publisher.

Death on Delivery
Paperback, Ebook
Publication date: November 2004
Price: $4.50 (ebook), $16.50 (paperback)
ISBN: 1931201609
Available from Twilight Times Books
http://www.twilighttimesbooks.com
To order: publisher@twilighttimesbooks.com

About the authors

Mayra Calvani is a reviewer, freelance journalist and the author of ten books for children and adults. She's a regular contributor to *Blogcritics Magazine, Suite101,* and the *Latino Books Examiner* for Examiner.com. Together with Anne K. Edwards, she co-edits *Voice in the Dark Ezine.* In addition, she's editor of *The Dark Phantom Review.* She lives in Brussels, Belgium.

To learn more about Mayra and her works, visit http://www.MayraCalvani.com. For her children's books, visit http://www.MayrasSecretBookcase.com.

Anne K. Edwards writes what she reads—mysteries. *Death on Delivery* is her second book, the first in the Hannah Clare series. Anne lives on a small farm in southern Pennsylvania with several cats and horses. Her interests other than reading and writing are meeting new people, traveling and talking to other authors. She is the editor of *Voice in the Dark,* a free monthly ezine featuring author interviews, columns, articles, short fiction, and resources for authors and readers. Visit her website at http://www.MysteryFiction.net.

CPSIA information can be obtained at www.ICGtesting.com
Printed in the USA
241696LV00001B/12/P